SCHÖNBRUNN farbig

Schönbrunn – in colour

Text and commentary: Georg Kugler

Photographs: Gerhard Trumler

162 illustrations, 91 of them in colour

English Edition

Edition Tusch Vienna

ISBN 3-85063-161-3

English translation from the German by Maria E. Clay
(essay, captions) and Bruce J. Turner (commentaries,
revised by Maria E. Clay)

Schutzumschlag: Haimo Lauth

During the Baroque epoch one idea especially captivated the imagination of both the aristocracy and the architects: the idea of the princely summer residence.

It was the embodiment of Baroque joie de vivre and of princely splendour, which, however, does not justify the conclusion that nothing but enjoyment and distraction was intended: it was also regarded as a mission and an obligation.

During the 17th century and until the mid-18th century the Baroque style took hold of all spheres of Europe's secular and spiritual culture and we may speak of an all-encompassing Baroque zest for life. This age of princely absolutism is the last one to derive its name without qualification from a concept borrowed from art history. The term 'baroque', which at first had been a negative and disapproving one, refers to the most salient characteristics of this style: movement and irregularity.

Indeed in poetry and music, too, the Baroque art forms are not an expression of harmony but rather of strength: by the powerful merging of all the arts this style seeks to create an almost intoxicating state, a heightened awareness of life, which in turn can be again experienced as harmony.

The Baroque style is to be understood as a response to the Italian Renaissance – not so much a countermovement but rather an enhancement. The criteria of genius are the same, as is the enormous fecundity and the wealth of talent which helped it evolve into a universal European style.

The fine arts of architecture, sculpture, and painting do not merely exist alongside each other but merge with one another – each of them can take the place of the others. From the buildings burst forth sculptural elements, paintings carry the sculptural wall decorations further or simulate them as they also fill the ceilings of the buildings with the illusions of the most daring creations of the architect. In Baroque art imagination in general plays a significant role, and designs and plans are as important as completed buildings. Fischer von Erlach's first design of the imperial summer residence at Schönbrunn – never executed because it was impossible to execute, but nonetheless a recognised masterpiece – contributed as much to the architect's fame as did any of his completed buildings. Baroque architecture dreams of boundless possibilities thereby revealing points of contact with the theatre and with music, both of which are capable of transcending the limits of space and time. It joins with them on festive occasions: triumphal arches, festive squares and stage sets become the setting for music and drama and for carefully choreographed ceremonial processions of "costumed" participants. The Baroque plays of the Jesuits, too, derived their effect from architecture and festival. Emotional stirrings that had been revealed for brief moments in a thoroughly theatrical world were subsequently immortalised through the medium of printing. The title pages of the books, however, resemble temple gates or triumphal arches. Even ephemeral events lasting not more than a few minutes, such as the magnificent fireworks, were not only prepared with great artistry, but also subsequently carefully preserved on copper plates as though it were a matter of immortalising some royal garden palace. For both phenomena are very closely connected and both were created by the same artists: the Baroque summer residence is unthinkable without its gardens, orangery, and pheasantry, the gardens without their waterworks, carousels, and fireworks, the festivities without the deliberate intention to impress contemporaries as well as posterity. The universal validity of the Baroque style brought about an unprecedented similarity between sacred and profane art. What to later generations seemed a profanation of the religious, Baroque painting and sculpture, such as the works of a Rubens or Bernini, was heralded at the time as the art of the new religiousness, calling people to the altar by rhetorical means similar to a sermon. This thoroughly Roman art, however, also glorified the absolutist prince and not only the Catholic one.

After the Thirty Years' War the protestant princes of Northern Germany, too, adopted the Baroque culture, although in a form that was modified and restricted by French rationalism, so to speak in a toned-down version, and very quickly moulded it in their own Germanic way. The countries of the Hapsburg empire, on the other hand, were receptive to Baroque art from its very beginning. Even at the height of the Reformation the Hapsburg dynasty felt committed to the Catholic church and the Spanish tradition. It carried the spirit of the Counter-Reformation and of the Baroque far into the 18th century. This fact also finds its expression in the large palatial monasteries in Austria such as Göttweig, Melk, Klosterneuburg, and St. Florian that belong to the *ecclesia triumphans* and yet are closely connected with the imperial concept. In no German city was the French influence as slight as in Vienna. It was the art and culture of Spain and Italy that were the decisive influences upon the residential city of Emperor Leopold I, who ruled for almost the entire second half of the 17th century, and they continued to be so during the reign of Charles VI.

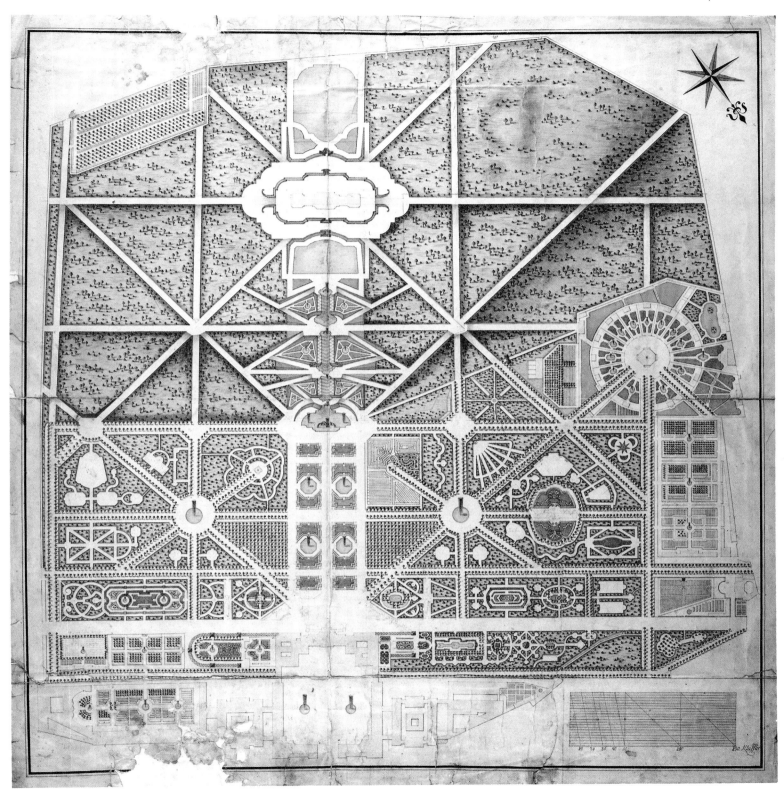

Plan der gesamten Anlage von Schloß und Park. Roman Anton Boos, 1780.
Layout of the palace and gardens. Roman Anton Boos, 1780.
Plan du château et du parc. Roman Anton Boos, 1780.
Planimetria generale. Roman Anton Boos, 1780.

Ansicht der Hofseite des Schlosses. Gemälde von Bernardo Bellotto, 1759.
View of the courtyard façade of Schönbrunn Palace. Painting by Bernardo Bellotto, 1759.
Vue du château de Schönbrunn du côté cour. Peinture de Bernardo Bellotto, 1759.
Veduta del castello di Schönbrunn dalla parte del cortile. Dipinto di Bernardo Bellotto, 1759.

XVI.Augusti. Anno M.D.C.CLIX.
Prussi cæsi ad Francofurtum ab exercitu Russo-Austriaco.

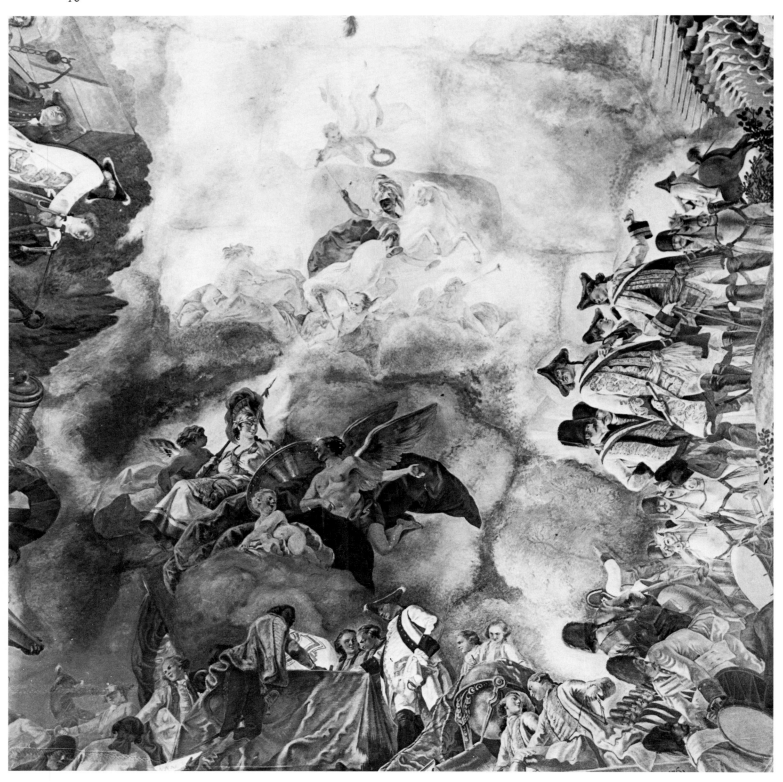

Deckenfresko in der Großen Galerie. Szenen aus dem Siebenjährigen Krieg.
Ceiling fresco in the Great Gallery, showing scenes from the Seven Years' War.
Fresque du plafond de la Grande Galerie avec des scènes de la guerre de Sept ans.
Affreschi del soffitto della Grande Galleria con scene tratte dalla guerra dei Sette Anni.

It was not until Maria Theresa that a Hapsburg ruler also spoke and wrote French – and the fact that she was more strongly influenced by the French spirit was at least in part due to her husband, Francis of Lorraine.

Her father, Charles VI, who was not able to permanently assert his claim to the Kingdom of Spain against the pro-French Party, had a dislike of France. This also emerges from a piece of advice which Prince Eugene of Savoy gave to a Lotharingian prince on the latter's arrival in Vienna: if he wanted to make a favourable impression on the Emperor, he should speak German with him and nothing but German.

Two events during the second half of the 17th century strengthened the German national consciousness and the feeling of solidarity of all Germans: the completely unprovoked occupation of the Imperial Free City of Strasbourg by Louis XIV in 1681 and the siege of the national capital of Vienna by the Turks in 1683. This second event, too, points up the intention on the part of France to obtain the hegemony in Europe and to break the worldwide leadership of the Casa de Austria. Although this leadership came to an end with the extinction of the Spanish line of the Hapsburgs in 1700, by then France had exhausted its resources and the heritage of world empire eventually passed to England.

After the relief of Vienna the Austrian triumph against the Turks and the French began. Misery and the plague were all of a sudden now followed by security and success! Self-confidence and splendour returned. Feelings of triumph combined with gratitude and found their expression not only in the Jesuit drama, but also in the monuments commemorating the end of the plague that were erected in city and market squares, in the construction of palaces and summer residences, in operas written by the Emperors and in "Steed Ballets". All of these are the expression of a highly theatrical world in which dignified Spanish manners combined with German coarseness and Austrian naturalness into Baroque joie de vivre. Surprisingly enough in Austria, and especially in Vienna, it was the architects who now had the greatest possibility of seeing their plans realised. For them the siege of the city by the sultan's army became a stroke of good luck, since the devastations by the Turks created an unprecedented demand for their services. The aristocracy soon vied with the Emperor in rebuilding the capital of the Empire. The Gothic town was now replaced by a new Baroque Vienna.

One of the Holy Roman Emperors who are hardly known to posterity is Joseph I (1705—1711), the eldest son and successor of Leopold I. When he died of smallpox in 1711, not yet 33 years old and after only six years as emperor, a monarch of outstanding ability and with him the greatest hope of a strong German Empire were buried, since the relief of Vienna in 1683 had been followed by an uninterrupted series of victories over the Turks, and the emperor's power now extended as far as the Balkans. The war with France seemed to have been decided in favour of the Holy Roman Empire through the several victories that Prince Eugene of Savoy, sometimes jointly with the Duke of Marlborough, had achieved against the French. Emperor Leopold's youngest son Charles had been King of Spain and the vast overseas possessions since 1703. Against this backdrop of power an artistic empire, too, could flourish. It was possible to continue a great tradition: during the almost fifty years of Emperor Leopold I's reign Vienna had become a center of musical drama; the imperial art collections were world-famous; the high

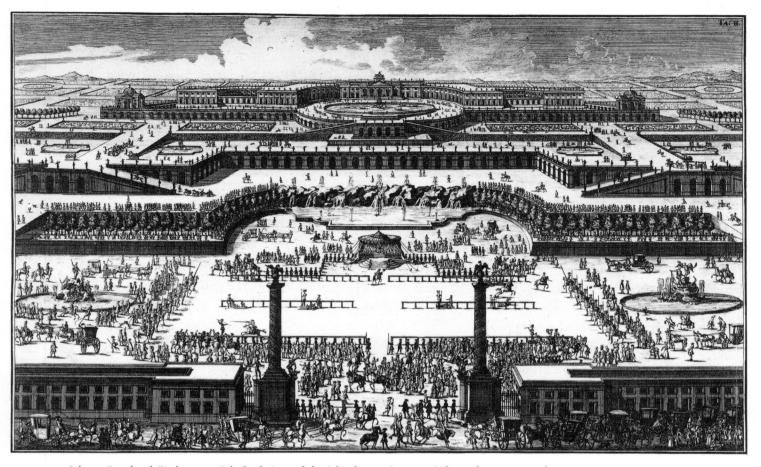

Johann Bernhard Fischer von Erlach, designs of the Schönbrunn Summer Palace, about 1693 and 1696.

aristocracy had been seized by an enormous desire to build after the Turkish siege had destroyed not only the imperial hunting lodge at Schönbrunn but many other buildings too. They had begun to build new palaces in the narrow streets of the city or summer residences outside the city walls. The fact that the palaces and gardens were filled with a life which in its sensual pleasures corresponded to the contemporary architecture, was graphically described in the famous sermons of Abraham a Sancta Clara and pilloried by the poet Wolf Helmhard von Hohberg, a member of the gentry of Lower Austria:

> *Litigating, gambling, building sumptiously/Being a guarantor, trusting much,*
> *Dressing beyond one's status/Having guests and giving banquets,*
> *Needless steeds, many dogs and greyhounds/other large domestic staff,*
> *Likewise eating, wantonness and love of sweet things/Make for empty kitchens, cellars, coffers.*

Such admonitions, however, did not curb what had become the greatest passion of the rich and powerful, whether of secular or clerical status: they happily continued to build. The most

distinguished member of the Austrian high nobility, Prince Karl Eusebius von und zu Liechtenstein, even wrote a *Work on Architecture (Werk von der Architektur)* in 1679, in which he stated that "Money is only good for leaving to posterity beautiful monuments in one's eternal and immortal memory."

Joseph, the energetic and active crown prince – like his father of a high and creative musicality and fond of all the arts – will have taken a lively interest in this splendid development, and all the more so, as since 1687 he was receiving daily lessons in architecture from Johann Bernhard Fischer von Erlach.

This appointment of Fischer von Erlach as teacher of the crown prince was of decisive importance for Austrian architecture. At the age of thirty the greatest architect of his time achieved a position which opened up the richest creative opportunities for him. In this politically as well as artistically so very important phase of German and Austrian history, about a decade after the siege of Vienna, Johann Bernhard Fischer von Erlach, the historically trained pupil of Bernini, designed his first and never executed plan for an imperial summer residence at Schönbrunn. The name derives from the "beautiful spring" (in German "schöner Brunnen") which was discovered

in the garden of the hunting lodge "Katterburg" that had been acquired already by Emperor Maximilian II in 1569. The spring, whose water was highly esteemed, was decorated with the statue of a nymph and the place was a popular attraction. Like the hunting lodge itself the extensive area of the deer-park and arboretum had been destroyed during the siege of Vienna in 1683. Now a new palace was to be erected there. Undoubtedly Fischer von Erlach's first design for this new summer residence was predominantly an expression of his own creative ability, but also of his royal pupil's ambitious plans – in 1690 Joseph had been crowned King of the Romans – who will not have been averse to the idea of an imperial residence on the hill of Schönbrunn.

Fischer planned a magnificent palace on the hill above the valley of the River Wien, approximately at the site where much later the "Gloriette" was built. From a large jousting field the walk was to lead up to the Emperor's residence by five extensive, artistically laid-out terraces with arcades, accompanied by cascades and fountains. Beyond the palace whose projected facade comprises 73 window axes (the present building has 39) was to stretch a seemingly endless park in the French style.

Fischer illustrated this design in his famous collection of copper plate engravings, *Entwurf einer Historischen Architektur* ("Plan of a history of architecture") in 1721 and remarked in the explanatory note that the view from the palace reached across the City of Vienna all the way to the Hungarian border – at that time the Leitha mountain range.

Let us leave open the question whether Emperor Leopold or his son ever really considered a realisation of this flight of fancy and eventually had to reject it only for financial reasons. Notwithstanding the impressiveness and artistic merit of Fischer's design in the *Historische Architektur* there was yet something colossal about it that is alien to the Austrian spirit. Who here in Vienna would ever have wanted a "German Versailles"? There was talk about that since people always make comparisons with other countries and peoples and with other rulers, in those days especially with hostile France. Despite the predatory wars the German princes in particular copied everything coming from the court of Louis XIV. The Hapsburgs, however, always regarded their position and the wielding of power more as a burden and a duty; they thought dynastically and did not put themselves into the centre. This is especially true of Emperor Leopold I. His son Joseph was somewhat more susceptible to the French personality cult and might have become a German Sun King. Therefore probably also Fischer's idea of crowning the second, executed plan of the palace with an equestrian statue of Joseph I, an entirely un-Austrian idea. The equestrian statues of the Hapsburgs up to that point had all been miniatures, masterpieces in bronze or ivory, unrivalled virtuoso pieces adorning the imperial art collections, but they were no monuments.

The second design by Fischer von Erlach was simpler in every regard and therefore more realistic. The palace has been moved down into the Wien valley and only the gradual northern slope of the hill has been turned into a park. In 1696 construction began according to this design.

At the end of the 17th century the royal summer residence had developed a typical form all over Europe, which is characterised particularly by two distinctive façades: a courtyard or city front and a garden front. The front facing the courtyard usually shows a staggered plan, indented in the middle, which might also be called horseshoe-shaped.

Die Gartenfassade des Schlosses.
The garden façade of the palace.
La façade du château sur les jardins.
La facciata del castello che dà sul giardino.

Brunnengruppe im Ehrenhof von Johann B. Hagenauer.
Fountain statuary by Johann B. Hagenauer in the Great Court of Schönbrunn.
Sculptures du bassin de la cour d'honneur de Johann B. Hagenauer.
Gruppo scultoreo nella fontana del cortile d'onore di Johann B. Hagenauer.

The wings which are normally offset – in Schönbrunn they are separate buildings – enclose the Great Court, the "Cour d'Honneur". Closed off by often magnificently wrought gates – as for example at the Belvedere in Vienna – it was used for the drawing up of the large six-horse state coaches; they had to pull up to perrons at the bottom of a broad flight of outdoor stairs. Festivities, too, could be celebrated here in the Great Court.

The garden front is much simpler and less divided; it shields the large expanse of a parterre, whose layout already indicates the arrangement of the entire park, in which Nature is transformed into architecture.

Architectonic main axes that run from the palace deep into the park were first conceived of in Renaissance Italy, although later the French landscape gardeners excelled in them. According to the French taste the gardens were to extend after the parterre either over falling or rising ground. We are familiar with such descending garden spaces as the settings of Watteau's paintings. The "Belvedere" of Prince Eugene has one of the most beautiful of these "descending" gardens, designed by Hildebrandt. In Schönbrunn, on the other hand, the landscape gardener had to deal with a terrain which rises quite sharply after a large level parterre. It took, however, several decades until the gardens were finally completed with the "Gloriette" in 1775.

At the end of the 17th and the beginning of the 18th century, however, one was grateful that the central portion of Schönbrunn Palace was finished enough to be shown to guests and to be lived in occasionally. Soon Schönbrunn became the scene of court receptions and festivities, and in June 1700 a great tournament took place in the palace courtyard, which had been designed for that purpose – "aux Courses et aux Carossels". Otherwise the entire building was still considered to be an imperial hunting-lodge, as may be seen from Fischer's designs. The woods rich in deer that surrounded Hietzing – around 1830 still called "the most beautiful village in Germany" – determined the purpose of the palace. The imperial deer-park at Lainz, too, was not far away.

Because of lack of funds the construction of the wings dragged on for many years, for the negative side of the Austrian heroic age were constant financial difficulties, which at the death of the court banker Samuel Oppenheimer in 1703 almost led to bankruptcy. The building activities were also delayed by the death of Emperor Leopold in 1705 and seem to have been entirely halted after the death of Emperor Joseph in 1711. However, the park and the waterworks had been completed by then, most probably by Jean Trehet, who had been working in Schönbrunn since 1705.

In 1711 the Emperor's youthful widow Wilhelmine Amalie inherited the palace. In 1728 she left it to her brother-in-law Charles and retired to the Salesian nunnery. Emperor Charles VI, however, was not particularly interested in Schönbrunn, not even after his power had been consolidated in Germany and Italy, and peace had been made with France at long last.

Although the Emperor was now in a position to build, he built eleswhere. He had new wings added on to the imperial town residence of the Hofburg, namely the imperial library, the winter riding school, and the wing housing the Chancellory, and had the "Stallburg" rebuilt to house the imperial picture gallery – at that time the largest one in the world. On the grounds outside the city fortifications extensive imperial stables were planned, which, however, were only built on a much smaller scale. Above all, Emperor Charles VI aspired to build a German Escorial, a truly

imperial residence, at Klosterneuburg. And finally there were other summer residences and hunting-lodges besides Schönbrunn, all of which had been more or less destroyed during the year of the Turkish siege. There was the "Favorita auf der Wieden", where Charles VI eventually was to die, which was the reason why his daughter Maria Theresa no longer wanted to live there and established the "Theresianische Akademie" there; then there was the "Augartenpalais", also known as "Favorita in der Leopoldstadt". This remained a ruin, but Jean Trehet, who had just been working on the gardens of Schönbrunn, had to restore the "Augarten" park from 1712 on.

It was not until a new generation entered the political stage, when the Archduchess Maria Theresa, who in 1736 had been married to Duke Francis of Lorraine, came to reign over the Hapsburg dominions in 1740, that the prospects brightened for Schönbrunn.

Maria Theresa's accession to the throne was only possible because of a dynastic law by which Charles VI had decreed by virtue of his imperial authority the female succession for his dynasty. By having been adopted by all the diets in the Hapsburg dominions, this "Pragmatic Sanction" received the character of the first constitution of the monarchy, and was still of importance as late as 1918. Of course the way in which this age was entirely caught up in a purely dynastic way of thinking and regarded kingdoms and countries as the private possessions of their rulers strikes us as strange today. During the last years of Emperor Charles VI's life, as the hope for a son dwindled, the recognition by the European powers of the female right to succession was the acknowledged aim of the imperial policy. Prince Eugene, however, was sceptical about these diplomatic and political efforts and kept insisting that a ready army and full coffers were more valuable than any treaties.

After the death of the Emperor it soon became clear that he had been right. The treaties were pieces of paper only and the twenty-three year old Archduchess, who was crowned Queen of Hungary at Pressburg before a year had gone by, found herself involved in war!

Thrift and cutting costs wherever possible became the order of the day. It is reported that the new monarch was shocked to find that the imperial kitchen was charging 4,000 guldens a year for parsley, or that the widowed Empress Wilhelmine Amalie, Maria Theresa's aunt (who had by then been widowed for thirty years) received twelve jugs of wine daily as a nightcap and each of her Ladies-in-waiting six!

From the very beginning Maria Theresa attended to every detail, even to the private affairs of her servants. Like no other monarch before her she gained an inside view of the business of the realm and the needs of the people, but often she could not see the forest for the trees. Her husband may have felt that he knew many things better, precisely because he knew less about many things, but Maria Theresa would not let go of even an inch of her power. Thus Francis had a very strange status indeed at court.

Although descended from one of the oldest and most noble families in Europe Francis had yet been nothing but a poor prince when in 1723 at the age of fifteen he was allowed to pay his respects to the Emperor's daughters in Prague. The Duchy of Lorraine, repeatedly conquered by France and occupied for decades, was at stake for the last time when in 1735 the young Duke Francis was to renounce his claim to his ancestral country in order to save the peace in the War of the Polish Succession. In the first instance Lorraine was to go to Stanislas Leszczyński, who in

turn would renounce the Polish crown, and later it would fall to the French King. As compensation the House of Lorraine was to receive Tuscany as soon as the last of the Medici had died. Francis agreed to this horse trade only under coercion; three times he threw down his pen, until Johann Christoph von Bartenstein, secretary of the Secret Conference, snapped at him, "No renunciation, no archduchess!"

Francis made the right choice. For all his life – whether as Grandduke of Tuscany, joint regent of Austria, or Emperor – he remained what he meant to Maria Theresa's heart, and that was much! Nevertheless she hardly let him get near any serious business of governing. He therefore soon looked for another field of activity which showed his talent: business. The Prince of Lorraine who had arrived in Vienna as a pauper died a millionaire.

At first, however, there was a dearth of money wherever one looked! But after Maria Theresa had passed the crucial test of the so-called first Silesian War against Frederick II, after the continued existence of the state had been secured and later on, on the death of the Wittelsbach Emperor, even the imperial title returned to the "House of Austria", efforts were made again to live up to the high reputation of the "imperial and royal" court.

In this desire rulers and subjects were united not only during the time of the Baroque. The monarchy and the state were regarded as one and the same, the private property of the prince and the property of the state were not yet distinguished, the honour and the prestige of the court were those of the state, of the nation!

The dignity of the monarchy demanded outward splendour. In a contemporary report we read (about Charles VI), "When the Emperor went for a ride, always accompanied by the imperial guard on horseback and on foot, with more than twenty state coaches, that spread an aura of truly imperial majesty!"

Along these lines generous plans were finally drawn up not only for completing the palace at Schönbrunn, but also for renovating it, whereby Maria Theresa herself wanted to make especially the decisions about the internal arrangement of the rooms. Somewhat maliciously Otto Christoph Count Podewils, the envoy of Frederick II of Prussia, later reported to his king: "She enjoys building, without understanding anything about it, a fact of which the house she had built at Schönbrunn to suit her own taste gives evidence." Indeed Maria Theresa often rejected plans that had already been approved. Her wishes for alterations angered the builders, and the results displeased those who were to live in the palace, above all her husband. But that he "could not hide his dislike", as is reported in the diary of the Lord Chamberlain of the Empress, Count Khevenhüller (1746), must not be taken too seriously, for his criticism was directed above all against the director of the imperial buildings, the Portuguese Count Emanuel Silva Tarouca. While Maria Theresa would discuss all building matters with the latter, her long-time mentor and confidant, she obviously did not ask Francis for his opinion. This had been the case from the beginning: not the Lotharingian architect Jean-Nicolas Jadot de Ville-Issey, whom Francis had favoured, had been entrusted with the building, but the young Nikolaus Pacassi, who had been born at Wiener Neustadt in 1716. In 1743, when the Austrians were victorious in their advances against the Bavarians and the French, he began to alter thoroughly both the exterior and the interior of the palace. Since Austria was only able to wage the war with the help of millions of

guldens provided by England, it was at that time that the rumour arose about Schönbrunn having been built with English subsidies.

Today we see the courtyard facade and the Great Court of Schönbrunn essentially as they took shape before Maria Theresa's own eyes and as Bellotto then painted them. The most drastic outward change of Fischer's building was the addition of a storey above the main floor. Since the Empress wanted to spend a good part of the year in Schönbrunn and moreover her family was much larger than that of her parents, she needed more living space. This need continued to increase over the years, for of the Empress' sixteen children ten lived into adulthood; the unmarried ones were to have five and the married ones ten rooms at their disposal whenever they were in Schönbrunn.

Last but not least more servants were also needed in the palace – each of the children was already surrounded by a small royal suite –, more guest rooms, and also functionally well thought-out state rooms that were equally suitable for family celebrations and for important state occasions. Pacassi therefore simply dismantled essential portions of the central part of the palace, and in place of the Great Hall extending from the court front all the way to the garden front and of its adjacent antechambers, he erected the two famous galleries. The Great Gallery overlooks the court and is reached by a large curved open-air flight of stairs, newly erected at that time, which leaves a five-gate driveway free. This feature was of importance in the new ceremonial. Whereas in the High Baroque the sixhorse state coaches were to draw up to the palace on wide ramps, in the Rococo they drove into the "sala terrena" of the building. From there staircases led upstairs. Pacassi created an extensive pillared hall on the ground floor and built the Blue Staircase by which visitors are led upstairs even today. It replaced a banquet hall of Fischer's palace, whose ceiling painting, which has been preserved and can still be seen, had been done by the famous Venetian Sebastiano Ricci soon after 1700. Parallel to the Great Gallery – and open to it through three arches – is the Small Gallery on the garden front, which is flanked by two Chinese Rooms, a round one in the west and an oval-shaped one in the east, both of which can also be reached by concealed staircases.

From a large balcony outside the Small Gallery two flights of stairs again lead down to the garden parterre. Thus Pacassi created a system of intricately linked and yet separable and thereby versatile state rooms as the central part of the palace.

Pacassi connected them to the wings by means of several stately rooms, some of which – for example the two antechambers to the left and right of the Great Gallery, the Eastern one of which is today called the "Carousel Room" – still show Fischer's plans, while others such as the Ceremonial Hall next to the Chapel in the East Wing were newly created by him.

While the facades of Schönbrunn were certainly not improved by the alterations, the new arrangement and design of the interior rooms is a masterly achievement of Pacassi. However, the Empress' influence on these alterations must not be underestimated. Her whole life long she took an active interest in the furnishing and interior decoration of the palace, spent large sums on it, and up to the year of her death she attended to the landscaping of the garden.

Pacassi's alterations were finished in 1749. Later the two galleries were altered again and were given segmental vaults, which were painted by Gregorio Guglielmi from 1760 to 1762.

It is remarkable that in these frescoes the imperial couple is portrayed completely naturally, without any kind of heroisation, as persons acting in a more or less historic situation. The conferring of the Military Order of Maria Theresa and the episodes from the Seven Years' War, which was still going on at the time the frescoes were being painted, are even depictions of current events. Maria Theresa had a remarkable sense of history: she had Martin van Meytens immortalise the major family and political celebrations, namely the marriage of her son Joseph to Isabella of Parma in October 1760 and his crowning as King of the Romans at Frankfurt in March 1764, in two series of paintings. Meytens and a number of painters from the circle of his pupils and his school began with the paintings immediately after the first event and worked on them from about 1761 to 1763 – i. e. during the same years that Guglielmi was painting the ceiling frescoes. After that they painted the coronation series, which unfortunately was badly damaged in the Second World War, so that today only the depiction of the coronation banquet in the "Römer", (a mediaeval building in Frankfurt that served as the city hall for centuries) can still be shown in Schönbrunn.

Recently, however, the restoration of the paintings of the festive procession of carriages entering Frankfurt and the coronation ceremony at St. Bartholomew's Cathedral has been undertaken. When finished the former painting will be on display as part of the Carriage Collection in Schönbrunn whereas the painting depicting the coronation ceremony will be exhibited in the Secular Imperial Treasury (Weltliche Schatzkammer) at the Hofburg.

It is remarkable that the Empress also commissioned her court painter Meytens to depict an event that had long passed, namely the ladies' carousel at the Court of Vienna on January 2, 1743. In addition to this painting a second one of the same group is today shown in the "Carousel Room", the depiction of the first awarding of the Order of St. Stephen's, which was established in 1764.

All of these paintings were probably intended for a Hapsburg pantheon which Maria Theresa planned to establish in the Belvedere Palace. Only when the latter was chosen for the imperial picture gallery in 1776 were the "historical paintings" brought to Schönbrunn. The wedding series ended up in the Ceremonial Hall, which in those days was called the "Battle Hall" – because of the large paintings of battle scenes that up to that point had adorned its walls.

An example of the romantic nature – still unusual in those days – of this interest in their own family history is the painting of the ruin of the original castle of the Hapsburgs in Switzerland painted by Joseph Rosa around 1765. It belongs to a series of Alpine landscapes with herdsmen and peasants which was housed in three rooms along the West garden front called "Rosa Rooms".

The "Room of the Horses", too, which leads from the oval-shaped room to the Ceremonial Hall takes its name from its paintings. Since Maria Theresa's time it has been adorned by a large painting depicting her uncle, Emperor Joseph I (1705–1711), and numerous companions coursing in the marshes of the River March near Vienna. The other paintings in the "Room of the Horses" were done by the famous court animal painter Johann Georg von Hamilton; they are painted on copper tablets and should properly be called horse portraits. In most cases they bear the name of the horse and its stud farm. In the imperial and aristocratic lifestyle this noble animal played a significant role as a faithful companion of the hero in war, and as a draught animal and parade

horse it was a splendid companion in the grand ceremonial parades, an indispensable living contributor to the festivities. Its stables looked like palaces, its looks were immortalised in portraits that were then assembled in horse galleries. One of the few that has survived to our day is the one in Schönbrunn. Extensive stables for the Emperor's own horses and the parade horses were of course also provided for in Schönbrunn. In Johann Bernhard Fischer von Erlach's design we see that they were supposed to be housed in the two separate buildings flanking the Great Court – "Ecurie pour 200 chevaux". To the left and right of the main entrance were supposed to be the coach houses for the state-coaches. It was only in Pacassi's design that the stables were altered into so-called "Cavaliers' Wings" and connected to the palace proper by means of arcades. He moved the stables and coach houses further west. In a part of these buildings and in the winter riding school, which was built later, the exhibition and the depots of the Carriage Collection have been housed since 1922.

We have mentioned already above that Empress Maria Theresa continued to take an active interest in the interior decoration of the palace throughout her life. Often alterations were connected with the larger or smaller repairs that became necessary over the years or else they were due to changes within the family.

One occurrence that greatly affected the life of the Empress was the unexpected death of her beloved husband, Emperor Francis I, in Innsbruck in the summer of 1765. The family had gathered there to celebrate the marriage of Archduke Peter Leopold to the Infanta Maria Ludovika. After his father's death "Pietro Leopoldo" as the second eldest son took over the rule of the Grandduchy of Tuscany, and the young couple therefore moved to Florence. As a consequence several rooms, among them those that had belonged to the "Retirada", i. e. the Emperor's private apartments, were completely remodelled. First and foremost in this connection we must mention the Vieux-Laque Room. The name in this case refers to Chinese and Japanese lacquer work, golden-coloured depictions of landscapes, gardens, flowers, and birds on a black background.

Rooms whose wainscoting with East Asian lacquer panels has been completely preserved have today become rare. Many such rooms were later altered, often because they showed some damage which it was decided not to have repaired; others were destroyed together with the palaces. In Versailles such suites were reconstructed only around 1950, using old panels. These panels, however, had originally come from the atelier of the Parisian lacquer artist Martin rather than from East Asia. The Vienna panels were acquired by Maria Theresa around 1770 for a very high sum. She loved such artwork more than diamonds, as she herself once asserted when the question arose of giving a valuable present to the influential Marquise de Pompadour. "There is nothing in the world", she said, "that I could not just as well do without, not even diamonds; only things that come from India, especially lacquer work and tapestries, do I really enjoy."

Maria Theresa loved the Vieux-Laque Room also for the family portraits set into the walls: portraits of her husband Francis I, her two sons Joseph II and Leopold II, and a number of grandchildren including her long-awaited first grandson Francis II, whose birth she had announced to her Viennese subjects from a box in the Hofburg Theatre with the words, "Hurrah, our Poldl has a boy!" The Million-Gulden Room, too, owes its fame to works of oriental art. In this case

they are Indo-Persian miniatures, important examples of Mogul art of around 1600. These were much sought-after collectors' items in Europe and as such already known to Rembrandt.

Interest in and preference for the culture and art of the Chinese and the entire Far Eastern world took hold of Europe a number of times: first at the end of the 16th century and then again at the beginning of the 18th. Chinese porcelain as the epitome of Chinese culture was always held in high esteem; it was collected, forged, and eventually manufactured in royal porcelain manufactories all over Europe, whose early products enjoy legendary fame and value with collectors as "Meissen", "Nymphenburger", "Alt Wien" etc. The dress style at court was influenced by the Chinese, and in the palaces Chinese objects of art were collected in suitably decorated rooms. The members of the court themselves dabbled in the practice of oriental art. Joseph's wife, Archduchess Isabella, is said to have designed the "Chinese" decorations of the Porcelain Room.

At this point we should like to remark that the visitor to a palace must not ignore or forget the way in which it was lived in and used. Apart from the fact that palaces were built for different purposes, the way they were furnished indicated whether they were used all year round or only occasionally. Although Schönbrunn had been designed and built as a hunting-lodge and occasional summer residence, after Maria Theresa's alterations it was regularly lived in from spring to late autumn. Usually the court moved from the Hofburg to Schönbrunn after Easter. The courtiers, especially the ladies, were not happy about it as we can read in Khevenhüller's diary. In spring 1752 he writes:

"On 5 April everything was ready to make the move to Schönbrunn; but as the weather has suddenly turned so much worse and it has even been snowing since last night, this morning I was given the order by the Empress to countermand the move until further orders, at fact about which those of us who do feel the cold, and especially the poor servants, were overjoyed."

While in Schönbrunn the life at court showed certain traits of a sojourn in the country; it was less ceremonious, more informal. As the Prussian envoy Count Podewils reported partly amused and partly critically, the Empress wanted to "live with the Emperor as though they were a bourgeois couple"; she wanted to be a model wife and a caring mother. No day was said to have passed without her seeing her children. She not only gave orders that "strict attention was to be paid to cleanliness" and emphasised that her children had been born to obey, and thus had to get used to this fact early on, but – unlike other personalities of high status – she also did not leave the entire physical and spiritual upbringing of her children exclusively to their tutors. And yet when it came to marriage all of them were sacrificed to politics. All had to enter into political marriages. In order to bring this about, close supervision and a well-regulated family life were necessary, which during one half of the year took place in Schönbrunn. It is for this reason that this palace is significantly different from the other great palaces. We are thus better able to understand the personal interest the princes and princesses took in the decoration of the rooms. Ink drawings by Emperor Francis and by his especially talented daughters Maria Christine and Maria Elisabeth are even set into the wainscoting of the Porcelain Room.

The royal dilettantism also turned to music and the theatre; living quarters and state rooms of the palace were to be filled with them. What would the court of a Baroque monarch have been without the theatre! Hence the regulations concerning theatre performances and who was

allowed to attend them were among the most important rules of the house that the Empress conveyed to the Lord Chamberlain Count Khevenhüller.

Since the days of the composing Emperors Ferdinand III, Leopold I, and Joseph I, Vienna had been the centre of musical drama. The poets, composers, theatre architects, and especially the singers were almost without exception Italians; one could almost have called Vienna the musical capital of Italy! Charles VI had inherited the outstanding musical talent of his forebears and like his father – although more sophisticated and superior – he was a great lover of the theatre. He produced operas himself and conducted them, whenever he was not sitting among the orchestra musicians. His teacher was Johann Joseph Fux, he brought Antonio Caldara to Vienna, tried to arrange for Goldoni to come, and when he met Antonio Vivaldi in Trieste in 1728 he was said to have talked to him more in a fortnight than to his ministers in two years.

Thus during the 18th century Vienna was able to retain its important position in music and it made the change in style from the grand festive Baroque opera to the German opera, the German Singspiel, on the strength of its own talent. Gluck, Haydn, and Mozart – music became the expression of the essence of this city.

Maria Theresa loved music and dancing, she sang beautifully and enjoyed it. She was fond of the theatre as is shown by her apt statement, "Theatricals are necessary, without them one cannot stay here in such a capital."

Let us quote from Carl Jacob Burckhart's fine essay on Maria Theresa, ". . . the Vienna in which Maria Theresa grew up was still part of a larger context of life ranging from Naples to Rome and Milan, to Brussels and Antwerp; Madrid still continued to belong to it in spirit, and that was the real world of Baroque culture, which is essentially Hapsburg and Counter-Reformation. All of this was festive, and nothing is more festive than Austria in the 17th and 18th centuries, than Vienna, at all times a festive encampment behind the front."

Aside from the court theatres in the city, there were also stages in the imperial palaces. The palace theatre at Schönbrunn built by Pacassi at the northwest corner of the Great Court at Maria Theresa's request between 1743 and 1747, now became the most important one. In the sixties, during the second major building period in Maria Theresa's time, it was redecorated by Hohenberg, the architect of the "Gloriette".

Apart from that plays were still performed in a more intimate setting in the Ceremonial Hall or in the Galleries. The theatre was an essential part of courtly culture: not only entertainment but also a display of imperial grandeur; not only watching with admiration, but also active participation. Maria Theresa and her sister Maria Anna had been urged to take part when younger, and the Empress did the same with her own children who repeatedly acted on stage.

Emperor Charles VI had appointed the famous Venetian poet Apostolo Zeno (1668–1750) court poet. In 1729 at Zeno's suggestion he also brought the Roman Pietro Antonio Metastasio (1698–1782) from Naples to Vienna. Although Metastasio could at first not get used to the "formalities of life at court" and the "noisy splendour" that reigned at the court of "the highest personalities on earth", he yet remained in Vienna to the end of his life. He shaped the artistic taste of the Emperor's two daughters, became Maria Theresa's favourite poet and was truly devoted to her.

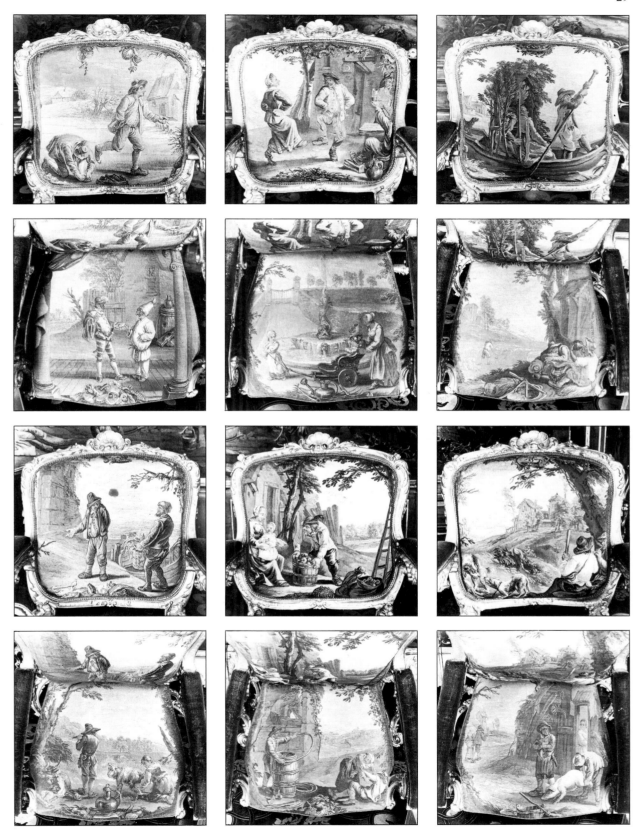

Gobelinsalon: Allegorische Darstellung der zwölf Monate auf den Sitzpolstern und Rückenlehnen der Fauteuils.
The "Gobelin" Drawing-Room: Allegorical representations of the twelve months of the year on the six arm-chairs.
Le salon des tapisseries: Les sièges et les dossiers des six fauteuils représentent les douze mois de l'année.
Salone degli arazzi: I sedili e le spalliere delle sei poltrone rappresentano i dodici mesi dell'anno.

Theateraufführungen in Schönbrunn mit Kindern Maria Theresias in verschiedenen Rollen. Gemälde aus der Schule Martin van Meytens'.
Theatre performances at Schönbrunn, with Maria Theresa's children in various roles. Paintings by the School of Martin van Meytens.
Représentations théâtrales à Schönbrunn avec des enfants de Marie-Thérèse dans différents rôles. Tableaux de l'Ecole de Martin van Meytens.
Rappresentazioni teatrali a Schönbrunn con alcuni figli di Maria Teresa in ruoli diversi. I quadri sono della scuola di Martin van Meytens.

Theateraufführung anläßlich der Vermählung Josephs II. mit Isabella von Parma, 1760. Gemälde von Martin van Meytens.
A theatre performance on the occasion of the marriage of Joseph II to Isabella of Parma, 1760. Painting by Martin van Meytens.
Représentation thèâtrale a l'occasion du mariage de Joseph II avec Isabelle de Parme, 1760. Peinture de Martin van Meytens.
Rappresentazione teatrale in occasione delle nozze di Giuseppe II con Isabella di Parma, 1760. Dipinto di Martin van Meytens.

Rösselzimmer: Das große Jagdbild von Philipp Ferdinand von Hamilton und vier Pferdeporträts:
Hermoso, Excellente, General, Philosopho.
Room of the Horses: The large painting of a hunting scene by Philipp Ferdinand von Hamilton, and four of the horse portraits:
Hermoso, Excellente, General, Philosopho.

Salon des chevaux: Le grand tableau de chasse de Philippe Ferdinand de Hamilton et quatre portraits de chevaux:
Hermoso, Excellente, General, Philosopho.
Stanza dei cavalli: Il grande quadro con scene di caccia di Philipp Ferdinand von Hamilton e quattro ritratti equestri:
Hermoso, Excellente, General, Philosopho.

Maria Christine – Peter Leopold. Martin van Meytens, 1750/51.

Peter Leopold – Karl Joseph. Martin van Meytens, 1759/60.

Maria Josepha – Marie Antoinette. Pierre Benevault, 1759.

Schönbrunner Doppelbildnisse.
Schönbrunn double-portraits.
Les portraits doubles de Schönbrunn.
Ritratti „doppi" di Schönbrunn.

Kaiser Franz I. und Kaiserin Maria Theresia bei der Gartenarbeit. Tuschzeichnung von Franz Walter.
Emperor Francis I and Empress Maria Theresa working in the garden. Ink drawing by Franz Walter.
L'empereur François Ier et l'impératrice Marie-Thérèse jardinent. Lavis de Franz Walter.
L'Imperatore Francesco I e l'Imperatrice Maria Teresa mentre si occupano di giardinaggio. Disegno in china di Franz Walter.

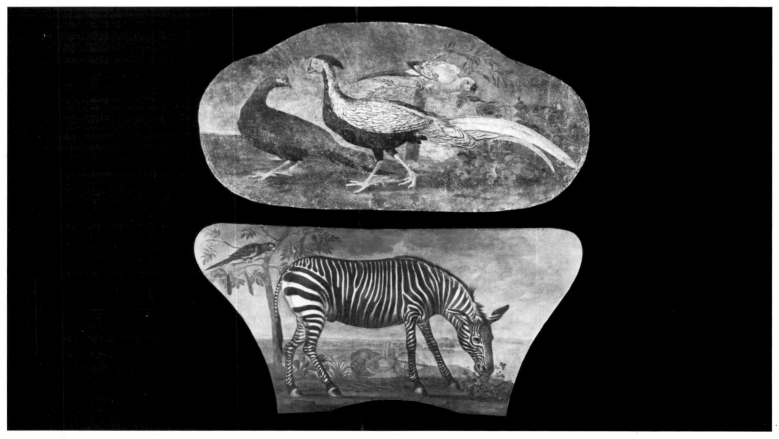

Tiergruppen von Johann Georg Hamilton, um 1735, und von Franz Fuxeder, um 1765.
Groups of animals by Johann Georg Hamilton, circa 1735, and by Franz Fuxeder, circa 1765.
Groupes d'animaux par Johann Georg Hamilton, vers 1735, et par Franz Fuxeder, vers 1765.
Gruppi di animali di Johann Georg Hamilton, intorno al 1735, e di Franz Fuxeder, intorno al 1765.

Of course he wrote in Italian, which was not only understood by all the educated people, but had practically become a second language for everyday communication in Vienna. It was Metastasio, who made the statement that the 52 German expressions which he had learned ought to be quite sufficient to save his life should the need arise. Metastasio is the author of a much-quoted ode "La deliziosa Imperial Residenza di Schönbrunn", but his real importance derives from his numerous poetic operas, for which Caldara, Wagenseil, Gluck, Haydn, and Mozart wrote the music. Thus the accepted hierarchy and sequence were, "The poet makes the drawing, the composer only colours it", as Gluck stated in his preface to "Alceste". Indeed, Metastasio's libretti were of great melodiousness and poetic expression, thereby foreshadowing the music.

Metastasio created a style of opera, characteristic of the imperial city at the time, that was closely connected with the phenomenon of the Baroque summer residence and the Rococo. In 1767, however, Gluck's "Alceste" was also premiered at the Palace Theatre at Schönbrunn – this was the second of his great reform operas, with which he broke away from Metastasio's style and created simple, noble characters in the classical sense for the stage. The libretto of this opera was written by the adventurous Calzabigi. Incidentally, in 1781 Mozart attended a performance of "Alceste" at the palace theatre of Schönbrunn.

Aside from the Italian literature French classical tragedy played an important part in the repertoire of the Court Theatres. It was not until Joseph II that an emperor was interested in German literature – to further it he founded in 1776 the German National Theatre in Vienna, later (and still today) known as the "Burgtheater". At Emperor Joseph's suggestion Mozart's "Abduction from the Seraglio" was first performed there on 16 July, 1782. His "Schauspieldirektor", on the other hand, was first performed in 1786 at the orangery at Schönbrunn after a festive reception given by the Emperor. Let us just briefly mention some other occurrences of importance for the intellectual history of the time that took place in Schönbrunn: encounters of the Empress with Lessing, Winckelmann, and with Gottsched, to whom she apologized for her poor German, although it was much better than that of Frederick of Prussia.

With Lessing she conversed about art and science, literature and the theatre, schools and education, and asked for his assessment of their development in Austria. It is part of the fascinating history of Schönbrunn that there the two perhaps greatest German personalities of the century conversed with each other, representing the North and the South of the realm respectively.

On the French example, an integral part of any large summer residence was the Baroque garden, the embodiment of Nature as ordered and shaped by the human mind. It, too, has its precursors in Italy. Renaissance man had found a new relationship to Nature and he admired the shells of sea animals, corals and sculptured specimens of ore, rhinoceros horn and ostrich egg, ivory, and the various tropical fruits. However, he collected them almost exclusively in a form fashioned by man, usually as imaginatively shaped vessels. The artistry of man "embellished" the marvels of Nature, "raw Nature" was ennobled by the human mind. It is with understanding for this attitude that we ought to approach the "French" garden. It is the monumental expression of this sense of order, which during the Baroque played an all the greater role since the 17th century was also the century of the great scientists and one believed already at that time that man could control Nature.

In the French garden, the greatest master of which was Le Nôtre, the landscape-architect of the park at Versailles, the various parts of the garden are optically connected with each other by long avenues that are laid out symmetrically to a main axis. Their plan consists of simple geometric shapes, as the expression of a logic which was regarded as the basis of truth and beauty. The points of intersection of the avenues are emphasised by basins with statues or fountains, the end points by buildings or statues.

The water rising from the ground is integrated into the design of the garden both in its still and its flowing form. Already Raffael had made use of the incline in the garden of Villa Madama for cascades. Baroque Rome then created the famous fountains that became exemplary. In many Baroque gardens there were canals and pools suitable for boating that became the scenes of grand or sometimes bizarre festivities such as water carousels, naval battles with musical accompaniment, tableaux vivants on floating islands, all of that also at night, further enhanced by fireworks.

In Schönbrunn for such festivities a link between the two Gloriette pools was planned in the form of a canal that would have run below the colonnades of the Gloriette. Special supply lines had to be built to feed the waterworks, but to this day the problem has not been solved satisfactorily, which is the reason why the waterworks of the Fountain of Neptune are only rarely to be seen in action.

As mentioned above, the first garden had been laid out at the beginning of the 18th century by Jean Trehet, certainly in accordance with Johann Bernhard Fischer von Erlach. Trehet interrupted his work and spent seven months in Paris in order to study French gardens. From this trip he brought back a thousand young trees and the model of a water machine.

At the time of Pacassi's alteration of the palace, efforts began to be made to extend the relatively small garden behind which the forest rose like a theatre backdrop, and to lay it out as Bellotto has painted it. Later on it was enlarged considerably, but fortunately it was not changed any more in the 19th century. Therefore to this day in Schönbrunn we can still receive the strong original impression of those stageset-like trees which were so ardently decried in the literary epoch beginning with Goethe and were almost everywhere replaced by the sentimental wilderness of the English landscaped garden.

The dark green, sharply outlined topiary walls have a certain magnificent air reminiscent of temple architecture, and yet one is aware that they consist of living plants.

Four major avenues cut across the park and divide also the flower parterre into square beds that are again divided by the central axis running from the palace to the Fountain of Neptune, which, however, as the last major accent of the garden lay-out, was not finished until 1781. At other prominent points, namely where the central or "linden" avenue intersects with the diagonals leading to the menagerie on the right and the obelisk on the left, basins were built at the beginning of the 1770's, in whose waters the well-known marble naiads by Wilhelm Beyer are reflected. Thus the creation of the garden took several decades.

In the meanwhile after the death of his father Joseph II had become Holy Roman Emperor and joint regent of Austria with his mother. He loved neither courtly pomp nor beauty that was devoid of purpose and usefulness. Of this fact his mother was very much aware, for in 1773 she wrote to her daughter Marie Antoinette in Paris, "I certainly understand that you cannot imagine

the changes on the hill of Schönbrunn. Also, they exist only on paper and will never be carried out. As you know the Emperor does not love Schönbrunn, and at my age it would be ridiculous to begin such a task. So far there is nothing on the hill, no building, I only had a large reservoir put at the top, so I can have a fountain facing the house at the end of the parterre. I am hoping that it will be functioning in two years; the parterre I plan to decorate with statues."

The Empress, however, obviously did not feel so discouraged for very long. In reality the further development of the gardens was very close to her heart, and in the following years it was continued in such a way that the young Emperor, too, warmed to it. To him the botanical garden and the menagerie were of considerable interest since they could fulfil instructional and educational purposes. Therefore from 1779 on the public was allowed to enter the park of Schönbrunn as well as the Augarten on the other side of Vienna. Something which in other cities was made possible only by later revolutions has been a matter of course to the Viennese since the days of Emperor Joseph II! The society at court, however, was none too happy that it was now to share the park with its inferiors. Their complaints to the Emperor were countered by his statement that if he wanted to be only among his equals he would have to spend his days in the Capuchin Crypt. (The Capuchin Crypt is the burial place of all the Hapsburgs.) Free access to the park of Schönbrunn also meant free access to the menagerie, and of all the parts of Schönbrunn this is the one most familiar to the Viennese from early childhood on.

The attitude of Emperor Joseph II is not only characteristic of his mind and character but also typical of his age. The philosophical and pedagogical movement of the enlightenment, which had originated in France, recognised that in the extensive collections of the royal houses and of the monasteries a significant part of Europe's cultural heritage had been preserved which was or ought to become the intellectual property of all the people and must therefore be accessible to all. Enlightened princes therefore donated their collections to newly founded schools or academies for instructional purposes. In accordance with the encyclopaedic ideal of education such institutions were also provided with a pharmaceutical garden, a fig-house or orangery, and a menagerie. Likewise collections of machinery, models, and tools were assembled in order to provide illustrative material for the students. All these endeavours were already included in Maria Theresa's reform programme; later she also made over her husband's substantial scientific collections to the state. In the overall concept of these collections of Emperor Francis the scientific portion of the park at Schönbrunn played an important role. One of the learned curators of his collections was the botanist Nicolaus Joseph von Jacquin (1727–1817), who undertook an expedition to South America and the West Indies from 1755 to 1759 the results of which benefited the botanical garden and the menagerie of Schönbrunn as much as the collections. Jacquin was born at Leiden and was thus Dutch like Maria Theresa's personal physician Gerard van Swieten. Both recommended to the Emperor the Dutch gardener Adrian van Steckhoven for the remodelling of the Schönbrunn gardens. His assistant was Richard van der Schot from Delft. Since the 17th century Holland had had a leading position in Europe with regard to floriculture and commerce. After all, Linné's binomial system for the classification of plants also began its scientific triumph from Holland. Small wonder, then, that the Schönbrunn botanical garden was called the "Dutch garden".

In the following decades, too, the head gardeners and directors of the menagerie undertook extensive and often eventful expeditions for collecting and studying purposes. As a result the area under cultivation was extended and new hothouses were built – called the "nursery and hospital of the Dutch garden"! By buying adjacent lots the area of Schönbrunn was extended west and south a number of times and the scientific part of it was enlarged. Thus today the zoological garden takes up the entire space of the former small pheasantry. In 1751/52 according to the plans of Jean Nicolas Jadot in the southwest corner of the park thirteen houses or sheds for animals were built in a circle around an octagonal pavilion. In front of them were paddocks for the animals with basins and planted with trees, each one separated from the others by high walls; on the side towards the pavilion they were enclosed by a fence.

This core of the historically so important zoo exists to this day.

Among the original animals at Schönbrunn were animals from the world-famous menagerie of Prince Eugene which had been dispersed after his death in 1736. Additional animals were acquired by expeditions, but also from itinerant menageries and as diplomatic presents. Whilst the first giraffe was brought to Schönbrunn from southern Africa by Georg Scholl in 1799, the second one was a gift of the Egyptian Viceroy in 1828.

Many of his descendants inherited the scientific-technical interests of Emperor Francis. In 1788 his son Joseph II extended the Dutch Garden by an arboretum on the terrain behind the parish church of Hietzing. There rare trees were planted, a few specimens of which can still be admired today. This Lotharingian interest in the natural sciences was especially marked in Joseph's two nephews, the later Emperor Francis II and the "Styrian" Archduke Johann.

Of the numerous new projects that were carried out over the decades, a systematic arrangement of 400 plants planted according to Linné's system of classification into genera, species, and subspecies based on an idea of Jacquin, and an "Alpine garden" in the Tirolergarten merit special mention. Both were intended for the botanical instruction and for the teaching of horticulture to the Archdukes, but also for the education of the public. A painting by Carl von Sales which shows Napoleon's son, Napoleon II, duc de Reichstadt, as a gardener reminds us that while growing up in Schönbrunn he, too, was urged to tend the garden, thus following a Hapsburg-Lotharingian family tradition.

In the second half of the 18th century in addition to the practical and scientific interest in Nature a sentimental feeling for Nature arose. As has already been mentioned, fortunately the park of Schönbrunn was not turned into an English landscaped garden. Instead Emperor Francis II had a magnificent garden of that kind laid out at Laxenburg Palace south of Vienna.

The park at Schönbrunn survived the Romantic Age that was not favourably disposed towards such parks and after years of neglect it was restored true to style and again well cared for in the second half of the 19th century. Typically for the age of historicism credit for this was due not only to a director of the gardens, but also to an art historian.

In the final analysis, however, it was really Emperor Francis Joseph I who saw to the preservation of the palace and the park. He again chose Schönbrunn as his residence during the summer months. There, where he had been born, he also spent much of his life, there he reigned – towards the end as the "hermit" of Schönbrunn.

The historical role of the palace seemed over when Emperor Francis Joseph died on the evening of 21 November, 1916. For more than two years he had no longer left the palace and the park. He who had said after the suicide of his only son and the assassinations of his wife and then of his designated heir that fate had spared him nothing had yet been spared one thing: to live long enough to witness the downfall of the large and powerful empire so dear to his heart.

With him a multi-national state passed away, whose variety and diversity were its undoing. In Schönbrunn the lights went out; it became a museum, a monument. And at first it was no glorified or admired monument either. For even in those that were deeply disappointed the memory was still fresh that Schönbrunn had become the embodiment of an unimaginative, rigid political approach that was not able to find a way out of the crisis that had led to the catastrophe. To be sure, Emperor Francis Joseph had realised what was at stake, but he was convinced of the inevitability of what was happening, while the military and the politicians were frivolously putting up with war in order to solve at one stroke the many problems with which the "Austrian question" was fraught.

The aged monarch had outlived his entire generation; without any personal contact to those around him he stood isolated at the helm of a state which he considered to be – in his own words – "an anomaly in today's world". For decades he had been essentially alone, because he did not understand or did not want to understand his closest of kin: not his ambitious, romantically inclined brother Ferdinand Maximilian (the emperor of Mexico), not his beautiful but eccentric wife Elizabeth, not his son Rudolph, who was torn between conflicting wishes and plans. In the last few years of peace in the monarchy, which might have been decisive for its survival he had also not achieved or even attempted to achieve harmony with his nephew and designated successor to the throne, Francis Ferdinand. From his own residence at Belvedere Palace the latter attempted to struggle against the aged Emperor in Schönbrunn and to gain influence. For that purpose he used the so-called "minor military chancellory" as a kind of shadow cabinet. Schönbrunn and Belvedere Palace, these two gems of Austrian architecture, became political catchwords, even terms of abuse, and this stigma stuck with both of them even after the catastrophe of 1918. It was only slowly that the image of the serene and cheerful Schönbrunn reemerged, that of a monument of high culture, a theatre of history. Today Schönbrunn again bears its name with the pride of that which is unique.

Escorial, Versailles, Schönbrunn. Whilst Spain and France may each be evoked by a single name, for multifarious and heterogeneous Germany at least Potsdam and Nymphenburg must also be mentioned. But Schönbrunn is more than they are, for it was the summer residence of the Emperor, designed and built in the age of the last imperial display of power and the last heyday of the old German Empire, and was subsequently the favourite residence of Maria Theresa, the monarch who created the Austrian state and fortunately was a decisive influence on it.

Schönbrunn is the embodiment of that Austrian Baroque which Wilhelm Hausenstein has compared to a current whose meaning and destiny it was to flow into that „motherly delta" into Maria Theresa.

Schönbrunn personifies the curious mixture of festivity and intimacy, of urbanity and pastorality, which wellmeaningly has also been called a characteristic of the Viennese way of life.

Schönbrunn is the graceful restingpoint in the memory of the hurrying visitor, to which his thoughts of Vienna, of Austria, are attached. Starting from this palace he roams through the history, art, music, and literature of this city, this country.

Schönbrunn is one of those great Baroque works of art that represent a synthesis of many arts, but its name has also an established place in political history. In it art and power combine into one concept in a way that is unrivalled except by Versailles.

Schönbrunn alone can stand comparison with the Bourbon Palace, which shaped all other European royal residences and outshines them, since its Hapsburg owners were always able to hold their own alongside and against France. Schönbrunn arose out of the historic and artistic strength of Austria, both of the Hapsburg dynasty and the country as such.

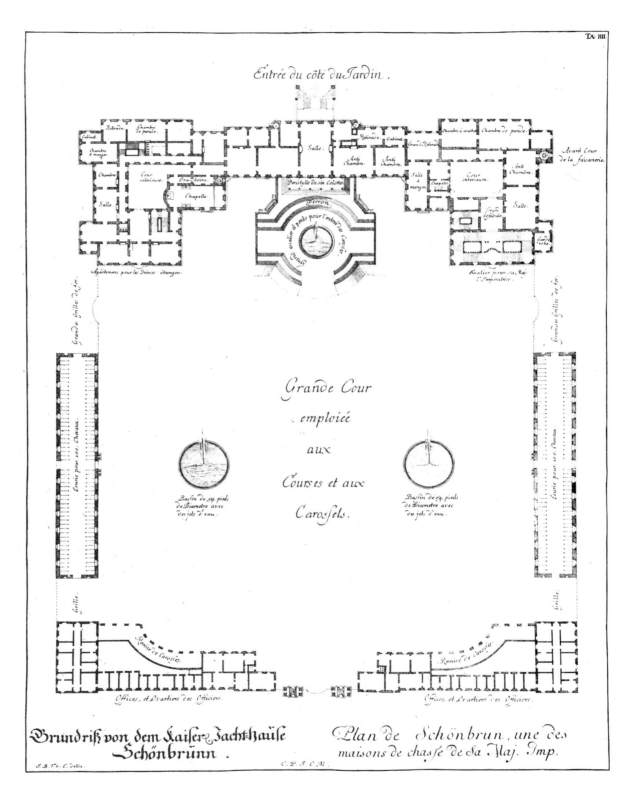

TA: IIII.

Entrée du côté du Jardin.

Grande Cour

emploiée

aux

Courses et aux

Carossels.

Bassin de 60. pieds de Diametre avec un jets d'eau.

Bassin de 24. pieds de Diametre avec un jets d'eau.

Grundriß von dem Kaiser Jacht-Hauße Schönbrunn.

Plan de Schönbrun, une des maisons de chasse de Sa Maj. Imp.

Grundriß des Schlosses nach dem Plan von Johann Bernhard Fischer von Erlach, 1696.
Plan of the palace as designed by Johann Bernhard Fischer von Erlach, 1696.
Plan du château de Schönbrunn conçu par Johann Bernhard Fischer von Erlach, 1696.
Pianta del castello secondo il progetto di Johann Bernhard Fischer von Erlach, 1696.

Erzherzogin Maria Theresia im Alter von zehn Jahren. Gemälde von Andreas Möller, 1727.
Archduchess Maria Theresa at the age of ten. Painting by Andreas Möller, 1727.
L'archiduchesse Marie-Thérèse à l'âge de dix ans. Peinture de Andreas Möller, 1727.
L'Arciduchessa Maria Teresa all'età di dieci anni. Dipinto di Andreas Möller, 1727.

Das Kaiserpaar Franz I. und Maria Theresia mit Familie. Gemälde von Martin van Meytens, 1754/55.
The imperial couple Francis I and Maria Theresa with their family. Painting by Martin van Meytens, 1754/55.
Le couple impérial de François Ier et de Marie-Thérèse avec sa famille. Tableau de Martin van Meytens, 1754/55.
La coppia imperiale, Francesco I e Maria Teresa con la famiglia. Dipinto di Martin van Meytens, 1754/55.

Das Frühstückszimmer in der Südwestecke des Schlosses.
The Breakfast Room in the southwest corner of the palace.
La salle du petit déjeuner dans l'angle sud-ouest du château.
Stanza della prima colazione nell'angolo a sudovest del castello.

Die Erzherzoginnen Maria Anna, Maria Christine und Marie Antoinette. – Nikolausbescherung in der kaiserlichen Familie, um 1760.
The Archduchesses Maria Anna, Maria Christine, and Marie Antoinette. – The imperial family celebrating the feast of St. Nicholas, circa 1760.
Les archiduchesses Marie-Anne, Marie-Christine et Marie-Antoinette. – La fête de la Saint-Nicolas dans la famille impériale, vers 1760.
Le Arciduchesse Maria Anna, Maria Cristina e Maria Antonietta. – La festa di San Nicolò presso la famiglia imperiale, intorno al 1760.

Die Kleine Galerie.
The Small Gallery.
La Petite Galerie.
La Piccola Galleria.

Das Spiegelzimmer und gelber Salon mit den Pastellen von Jean Etienne Liotard.
The Room of Mirrors and the Yellow Drawing-Room with the pastels by Jean Etienne Liotard.
La salle des glaces et le salon jaune avec les pastels de Jean Etienne Liotard.
La Stanza degli Specchi e il Salone Giallo con i quadri di Jean Etienne Liotard.

Die Große Galerie; Kaiserin Maria Theresia und der von ihr gestiftete militärische Verdienstorden.
The Great Gallery; Empress Maria Theresa and the military decoration founded by her.

La Grande Galerie; l'impératrice Marie-Thérèse et l'ordre du mérite qu'elle a créé.
La Grande Galleria; l'Imperatrice Maria Teresa e l'ordine al merito da lei istituito.

Öffentlicher Einzug der Prinzessin Isabella von Parma als Braut des Erzherzogs Joseph II. in Wien, 1760. Gemälde von Martin van Meytens.
Festive carriage procession of Princess Isabella of Parma entering Vienna as the bride of Archduke Joseph II, in 1760. Painting by Martin van Meytens.
Entrée solenelle de la princesse Isabelle de Parme comme fiancée de l'archiduc Joseph II, à Vienne en 1760. Peinture de Martin van Meytens.
Ingresso ufficiale a Vienna della Principessa Isabella di Parma, sposa dell'Arciduca Giuseppe II (1760). Dipinto di Martin van Meytens.

Wagenburg: Prinzengalawagen und Imperialwagen mit dazugehörigem Gespann.
Carriage Collection: Princely gala coach and imperial coach with their team.
Musée des voitures: Les carrosses princiers de gala et le carrosse impérial avec son attelage.
Museo delle carrozze: Carrozze principesche di gala e carrozza imperiale con pariglia di cavalli.

Maria Theresia bei der ersten Verleihung des St.-Stephans-Ordens, 1764. – Damenkarussell des Wiener Hofes, 1743. Gemälde von Martin van Meytens.
Maria Theresa awarding the Order of St. Stephen's, 1764. – The Ladies' Carousel at the Court of Vienna, 1743. Paintings by Martin van Meytens.
Marie-Thérèse à la investiture de l'ordre de Saint-Etienne, 1764. – Carrousel des dames de la Cour de Vienne, 1743. Tableaux de Martin van Meytens.
Maria Teresa durante il conferimento dell'ordine civile di Santo Stefano, 1764. – Corteo a cavallo delle dame, 1743. Dipinti di Martin van Meytens.

Die Chinesischen Zimmer: Japanische Porzellanvasen, Rokokodekorationen.
The two Chinese Rooms: Japan porcelain vases, Rococo decorations.
Les salons chinois: Vases en porcelain japonais, decorations rococo.
Salottini cinese: Vasi di porcellana giapponese, decorazione rococò.

Das Runde Chinesische Zimmer.
The Round Chinese Room.
Le cabinet chinois rond.
Il salottino cinese rotondo.

Das Vieux-Laque-Zimmer mit den Bildnissen von Batoni und Maron. – The "Vieux-Laque" Room with the portraits by Batoni and Maron.

Le salon Vieux-Laque avec les portraits de Batoni et Maron. – La stanza vieux-laque con i ritratti di Batoni e Maron.

58

Das Millionenzimmer und die indopersischen Miniaturen. – The "Million Gulden Room" with its Indo-Persian miniatures.

Le salon des millions et les miniatures indo-persanes. – La stanza dei milioni e le miniature indopersiane.

Der Blaue oder Chinesische Salon.
The Blue or Chinese Drawing-Room.
Le salon bleu ou salon chinois.
Il salone azzurro o cinese.

Das Große Rosa-Zimmer mit einem Porträt der Kaiserin Maria Theresia.
The Large Rosa Room with a portrait of Empress Maria Theresa.
Le grand salon de Rosa avec un portrait de l'impératrice Marie-Thérèse.
La grande stanza di Rosa con un ritratto dell'Imperatrice Maria Teresa.

64

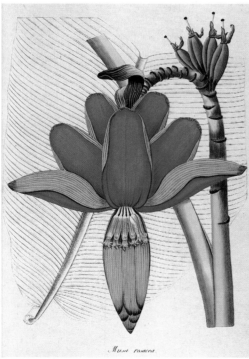

Illustrationen aus einem wissenschaftlichen Werk des Botanikers Nicolaus Joseph von Jacquin. – Wandmalereien in den Bergl-Zimmern.
Illustrations from a scientific work by the botanist Nicolaus Joseph von Jacquin. – Murals by Johann Bergl (Bergl Rooms).
Illustrations provenant d'un ouvrage scientifique du botaniste Nicolaus Joseph von Jacquin. – Peintures murales dans les salles de Bergl.
Illustrazioni da un'opera scientifica del botanico Nicolaus Joseph von Jacquin. – Affreschi delle stanze di Bergl.

Maria Ludovica von Toskana mit ihren Kindern. Anton von Maron, 1770. – Peter Leopold von Toskana und sein Bruder, Joseph II. Pompeo Batoni, 1769.
Maria Ludovica of Tuscany and her children. Anton von Maron, 1770. – Peter Leopold of Tuscany and his brother, Joseph II. Pompeo Batoni, 1769.
Marie Ludovica de Toscane avec ses enfants. Anton von Maron, 1770. – Pierre Leopold de Toscane et son frére, Joseph II. Pompeo Batoni, 1769.
Maria Ludovica di Toscana con i figli. Anton von Maron, 1770. – Pietro Leopoldo di Toscana e suo fratello, Giuseppe II. Pompeo Batoni, 1769.

Die Gartenseite des Schlosses. Gemälde von Bernardo Bellotto, um 1760. – Details aus den Wandmalereien der Bergl-Zimmer.
The garden façade of Schönbrunn Palace. Painting by Bernardo Bellotto, c. 1760. – Details from the murals in the Bergl Rooms.
Le château côté jardin. Tableau de Bernardo Bellotto, vers 1760. – Détails de peintures murales des salles de Bergl.
Facciata del castello vista dal giardino. Dipinto di Bernardo Bellotto, intorno al 1760. – Affreschi nelle stanze di Bergl. (Particolari).

Die Nymphe Egeria am „Schönen Brunnen" und der Najadenbrunnen im östlichen Rundbassin von Wilhelm Beyer.
The nymph Egeria at the "Beautiful Spring" and the Fountain of the Naiad in the eastern round basin, both by Wilhelm Beyer.

La nymphe Egérie à la „Belle Fontaine" et la fontaine des naïades dans le bassin rond oriental de Wilhelm Beyer.
La ninfa Egeria seduta alla sorgente d'acqua „Bella Fontana" e la fontana delle Najadi nella piscina rotonda di Wilhelm Beyer.

Der „französische" Park mit Skulpturen und mit der „Römischen Ruine" von Ferdinand von Hohenberg, um 1775.
The "French" park with statuary and with the "Roman Ruin" by Ferdinand von Hohenberg, c. 1775.
Le parc „à la française" avec des sculptures et avec la „ruine romaine" de Ferdinand de Hohenberg, vers 1775.
Il parco „francese" con sculture e con le „Rovine Romane" di Ferdinand von Hohenberg, intorno al 1775.

Der Kammergarten des Kaisers Franz Joseph an der Westfront des Schlosses.
The private garden of Emperor Francis Joseph along the west façade of the palace.
Le jardin de la Cour de l'empereur François-Joseph du côté de la façade occidentale du château.
Il giardino di Corte dell'Imperatore Francesco Giuseppe sul fronte ovest del castello.

Der Kammergarten.
The imperial family's private garden.
Le jardin de la Cour.
Il giardino di Corte.

Pavillon und Rosenhag im Kronprinzengarten vor der Ostfassade. – Das Palmenhaus, errichtet 1881.
Pavilion and rose hedge in the "Garden of the Crown Prince" along the east façade of the palace. – The Palm House was built in 1881.
Pavillon et roseraie dans le jardin du prince héritier devant la façade orientale. – La grande serre à palmiers, construite en 1881.
Padiglione e roseto nel giardino del Principe ereditario di fronte alle facciata est. – La serra di palme costruita nel 1881.

Äneas rettet Vater und Sohn aus dem brennenden Troja. Statue im Gartenparterre. – Detail vom Neptunbrunnen. – Der Garten im Winter.
Aeneas with father and son fleeing from burning Troy. Sculpture in the garden parterre. – Detail from Fountain of Neptune. – The garden in winter.

Enée sauve son père et son fils de l'incendie de Troie. Statue dans le parterre du jardin. – Détail de la fontaine de Neptune. – Le jardin en hiver.
Enea che salva il padre ed il figlio dalle fiamme di Troja. Statua nel parterre del giardino. – La fontana di Nettuno. – Il giardino nell' inverno.

Ausblick aus der Kleinen Galerie: Die Gloriette, errichtet 1775 nach Plänen Ferdinand von Hohenbergs.
View of the Gloriette from the Small Gallery. The Gloriette, designed by Ferdinand von Hohenberg, was built in 1775.
Vue de la Petite Galerie: la Gloriette, construite en 1775 d'après les plans de Ferdinand de Hohenberg.
Veduta dalla Piccola Galleria: La Gloriette, costruita nel 1775 secondo in progetti di Ferdinando von Hohenberg.

Trophäen. Bildhauerarbeiten Johann B. Hagenauers an den Treppen der Gloriette.
Trophies. Sculptures by Johann B. Hagenauer, flanking the stairs of the Gloriette.
Trophées. Travaux du sculpteur Johann B. Hagenauer sur les escaliers de la Gloriette.
Trofei. Opere scultoree di Johann B. Hagenauer all'inizio della scalinata che porta alla Gloriette.

Der Herzog von Reichstadt, Sohn Napoleons I. Gemälde von Carl von Sales, um 1820. – Sein Gartenwagen ist in der Wagenburg zu sehen.
Napoleon II, Duc de Reichstadt, son of Napoleon I. Painting by Carl von Sales, c. 1820. – His garden carriage is exhibited in the Carriage Collection.
Le duc de Reichstadt, fils de Napoléon Ier. Portrait de Carl von Sales, vers 1820. – On peut voir son phaéton au musée des Voitures impériales.
Il Duca di Reichstadt, figlio di Napoleone I. Dipinto di Carl von Sales, intorno al 1820. – Il suo carrozzino si può ammirare nel Museo delle carrozze.

„Moldau und Elbe" von Wilhelm Beyer, 1776; allegorische Figurengruppe im Bassin vor der „Römischen Ruine".
"The Moldau and the Elbe" by Wilhelm Beyer, 1776; allegorical statuary group in the basin in front of the "Roman Ruin".
„La Moldau et l'Elbe" de Wilhelm Beyer, 1776; groupe de figures allégoriques dans le bassin devant la „ruine romaine".
„Moldava ed Elba" di Wilhelm Beyer, 1776. Gruppo allegorico nella piscina di fronte alle „Rovine Romane".

Kaiser Franz Joseph I. in der Galauniform eines österreichischen Feldmarschalls. Gemälde von Anton Einsle, 1848. – Kaiserin Elisabeth in einer großen Robe. Gemälde von Franz Ruß, 1863.

Emperor Francis Joseph I in the gala uniform of an Austrian field-marshal. Painting by Anton Einsle, 1848. – Empress Elizabeth wearing a festive robe. Painting by Franz Russ, 1863.

L'empereur François-Joseph Ier portant l'uniforme de gala d'un feld-maréchal autrichien. Tableau de Anton Einsle, 1848. – L'impératrice Elisabeth en robe de gala. Tableau de Franz Russ, 1863.

L'Imperatore Francesco I in alta uniforme di un feldmaresciallo austriaco. Dipinto di Anton Einsle, 1848. – L'Imperatrice Elisabetta in abito di gala. Dipinto di Franz Russ, 1863.

Das Hundertjahr-Jubiläum des Maria-Theresien-Ordens 1857. Der Kaiser auf der Schloßtreppe. Gemälde von Fritz d'Allemand.
The centennial of the founding of the Order of Maria Theresa in 1857. The Emperor descending the palace stairway. Painting by Fritz d'Allemand.
Le centenaire de l'ordre de Marie-Thérèse 1857: L'empereur sur l'escalier du château. Peinture de Fritz d'Allemand.
Centenario della fondazione dell'ordine di Maria Teresa 1857. L'imperatore sullo scalone del castello. Dipinto di Fritz d'Allemand.

Festbankett für die Ritter des Maria-Theresien-Ordens in der Großen Galerie des Schlosses. Gemälde von Fritz d'Allemand, 1857.
Banquet in the Great Gallery of Schönbrunn honouring the Knights of the Order of Maria Theresa. Painting by Fritz d'Allemand, 1857.

Banquet de gala pour les chevaliers de l'ordre de Marie-Thérèse dans la Grande Galerie du château. Tableau de Fritz d'Allemand, 1857.
Banchetto ufficiale per i cavalieri dell'ordine militare di Maria Teresa nella Grande Galleria del castello. Dipinto di Fritz d'Allemand, 1857.

Erläuterungen – Commentaries – Commentaires – Descrizioni

Erläuterungen

8/9   Ansicht der Hofseite des Schlosses. Gemälde von Bernardo Bellotto, 1759.

Der Venezianer Bernardo Bellotto (1721–1780) hatte bei seinem Onkel Antonio Canal die Vedutenmalerei erlernt, jene Kunst, die eine sachlich getreue Wiedergabe einer Stadt oder Landschaft mit der Forderung nach bildmäßiger Gestaltung verbindet. Wie sein Onkel nannte auch er sich Canaletto, trat aber nur kurze Zeit in dessen Fußstapfen und verließ 1747 Italien für immer. Er wirkte fast zwei Jahrzehnte in Dresden, dann von 1767 bis zu seinem Lebensende in Warschau. In den Jahren 1759 und 1760, während die Preußen seine zweite Heimat Dresden belagerten und bombardierten, arbeitete er in Wien, und zwar hauptsächlich für den Kaiserhof. Die damals entstandenen Ansichten der Stadt und der Schlösser zeigen in erster Linie Plätze, Gebäude und Anlagen, die während der gerade vergangenen Jahrhunderthälfte entstanden waren. Es war also das „moderne Wien" von 1760, das Bellotto getreulich festhielt, und da durfte Schönbrunn nicht fehlen!
Der Maler hat den großen Ehrenhof des Schlosses von Menschen belebt dargestellt. Seine „Staffagefiguren" sind sehr oft charakteristisch für einen Platz und lebensnah erfaßt. Hier aber ist ein historisches Ereignis festgehalten, das ganz Wien in Begeisterung versetzte: Feldmarschalleutnant Laudon hatte am 12. August 1759 bei Kunersdorf östlich der Oder einen großen Sieg über Friedrich II. von Preußen errungen. In Khevenhüllers Tagebuch liest man darüber: „Den 16. (August) fuhren Ihre Majestäten um halb 11 Uhr zu den Augustinern auf der Landstraße wegen des S. Rochifestes. Bei unserer Zuruck-Kunfft ritte der Obristleutnant vom Löwensteinischen Chevauxlégers (-Regiment) Graf Joseph Kinski ... mit 20 Blasenden und 4 Postmeistern ein und überbrachte den Bericht des General Laudon von obbemelter Victori."
Das Bild befindet sich im Kunsthistorischen Museum.

12/13   Johann Bernhard Fischer von Erlach, Entwürfe für das kaiserliche Lustschloß Schönbrunn, ca. 1693 und 1696.

Johann Bernhard Fischer von Erlach (1656–1723) hat im Jahre 1721, als der „große alte Mann" der deutschen Architektur, einen Band mit großen Kupferstichen publiziert, den er „Entwurf einer historischen Architektur" nannte. In diesem Werk gibt Fischer einen Überblick über die Baukunst seit der Antike, mit Rekonstruktionen der frühesten Großbauten der Menschheit, und stellt zuletzt seine eigenen Werke dar.
Zu diesen zählt er auch das erste, nicht ausgeführte Projekt für Schönbrunn, das er in der Bildunterschrift „Venérie Imperiale" nennt, also kaiserliches Jagdhaus: Zu dem riesigen Lustschloß auf der Anhöhe des Schönbrunner Berges führen kunstvoll angelegte Rampen hinauf, die von sechsspännigen Karossen befahren werden konnten. Im Vordergrund reicht ein großer Fest- und Turnierplatz mit einem prächtigen Zelt für den Kaiser und seine Gäste bis an das breite Tor, das von Säulen flankiert ist. Sie tragen schon Adler, wie sie heute die Obelisken zu beiden Seiten des Tores krönen.
Im zweiten Entwurf weicht das phantasievolle, ja phantastische

Commentaries

8/9   View of the courtyard façade of Schönbrunn Palace. Painting by Bernardo Bellotto, 1769.

The Venetian Bernardo Bellotto (1721–1780) had learned the art of painting vedutas, which combine the objective and naturalistic depiction of a city or landscape with the demands of balanced composition, from his uncle, Antonio Canal. Although he called himself Canaletto after his uncle, Bellotto followed in his uncle's footsteps only briefly before leaving Italy permanently in 1747. Thereafter he resided in Dresden for almost two decades before moving to Warsaw in 1767, where he remained until the end of his life. In the years 1759 and 1760, while the Prussians were besieging and bombarding his second home, Dresden, Bellotto came to Vienna, where he worked primarily in the service of the emperor. The views of the city and its palaces painted during that time include, above all, the squares, buildings, and grounds that traced their origins to the first half of the 18th century. The subject of Bellotto's representations was the "modern Vienna" of 1760 – from which Schönbrunn could not be missing!
The artist's portrayal of the courtyard of the palace is invigorated by human life; his "staffage" figures are very often typical of a locality and naturalistically represented. In this case Bellotto has recorded a historical event that had all of Vienna at fever pitch: Lieutenant Field Marshal Laudon had won an important battle over Friedrich II of Prussia near Kunersdorf on 12th August 1759. In Khevenhüller's journal one can read: "On the sixteenth (of August), at half past ten, His Majesty was driving to the Augustinians on Landstraße for the feast of St. Rochus. Upon our return the Lieutenant Colonel of the Chevauxléger Regiment of Löwenstein, Count Joseph Kinski, arrived ... with twenty trumpeters and four postilions to proclaim the news of General Laudon's victory."
The picture is in the Kunsthistorisches Museum, Vienna.

12/13   Johann Bernhard Fischer von Erlach, designs of the Schönbrunn Summer Palace, about 1693 and 1696.

As the "grand old man" of German architecture, Johann Bernhard Fischer von Erlach (1656–1723) published a volume of large copperplate engravings in 1721 titled, "Entwurf einer historischen Architektur." In it Fischer surveys the development of architecture since antiquity, reconstructing man's earlier accomplishments before going on to present his own designs.
Included among these is his first design for an imperial huntinglodge at Schönbrunn, subtitled the "Venérie Imperiale", which was never executed. Artfully arranged ramps which were capable of supporting coaches drawn by teams of six horses lead to the gigantic summer palace on the crest of the rise. In the foreground the expansive parade- and tournament-ground, including a splendid tent for the emperor and his guests, extends all the way to the wide gateway arch flanked by columns. The latter are surmounted by eagles similar to those found today atop the obelisks on both sides of the gateway. The second design has given way to reality; Fischer von Erlach has moved the palace down into the valley. The view of the facade facing the Great Court and the ground-plan he also published do include, however, all the details of the plan that was accepted in 1696 by

Commentaires

8/9 Vue du château de Schönbrunn du côté cour. Peinture de Bernardo Bellotto, 1759.

Le vénitien Bernardo Bellotto (1721–1780) avait appris chez son oncle Antonio Canal la peinture de perspectives, cet art qui unit une reproduction fidèle à la réalité d'une ville ou d'un paysage aux exigences de l'art pictural. Comme son oncle, il se nomma Canaletto mais quitte l'Italie pour toujours en 1747. Il exerça son activité presque une vingtaine d'années à Dresde puis de 1767 jusqu'à la fin de sa vie, à Varsovie. En 1759/60, alors que les Prussiens assiégeaient et bombardaient Dresde, sa deuxième patrie, il travailla à Vienne et principalement, pour la cour impériale. Les vues de la ville et des châteaux qu'il peignit alors montrent en premier lieu les places, les monuments et les parcs qui avaient été construits justement pendant la première moitié du siècle. C'est donc la „Vienne moderne" de 1760 que Bellotto peignit fidèlement et il ne pouvait manquer de peindre Schönbrunn!

Il a représenté la grande „cour d'Honneur" du château animée par des personnages. Ses „figures" sont souvent très caractéristiques d'un endroit et sont très proches de la réalité. Mais ici, il a fixé par l'image un évènement historique qui enthousiasma tout Vienne; le feld-maréchal Laudon avait remporté une grande victoire le 12 août 1759 à côté de Kunersdorf à l'est de l'Oder sur Frédéric de Prusse. Dans le journal de Khevenhüller, on peut lire à ce sujet; „Le 16 (août), leurs Majestés se rendirent vers dix heures et demie au couvent des Augustins à cause de la fête de Saint-Roch. Lors de notre retour, le comte Joseph Kinski, lieutenant-colonel du régiment de chevaux-légers de Löwenstein, arriva à cheval avec 20 clairons et 4 courriers et remit la lettre du général Laudon annonçant la victoire".

Le tableau se trouve au musée des Beaux-arts.

12/13 Johann Bernhard Fischer von Erlach, les plans du château imperial de plaisance de Schönbrunn, vers 1693 et 1696.

Johann Bernhard Fischer von Erlach (1656–1723) a publié en 1721 un livre avec de grandes gravures sur cuivre qu'il nomma „Esquisse d'une histoire de l'architecture". Dans cet ouvrage, Fischer von Erlach donne une idée d'ensemble de l'architecture depuis l'Antiquité et présente ses propres œuvres à la fin de l'ouvrage.

Il y inclut aussi le premier projet pour Schönbrunn qui ne fut pas réalisé; il lui donne comme légende „Vénerie Imperiale", c'est-à-dire pavillon de chasse impérial: des rampes aménagées avec art conduisent au palais de plaisance de dimension géantes qui s'élève au sommet de la colline de Schönbrunn. Au premier plan, il y a une grande place des fêtes et de tournoi qui s'étend jusqu'à la large porte flanquée de colonnes. Elles portent déjà un aigle comme celui qui aujourd'hui couronne les obélisques des deux côtés de la porte.

Le deuxième plan est plein d'imagination; il en déborde même car il s'écarte de la réalité. On peut dire, si on peut s'exprimer ainsi, que Fischer von Erlach a fait descendre le château de la colline. La vue du côté de la cour d'Honneur et le plan d'ensemble nous permettent de reconnaitre tous les détails du plan qui fut accepté comme base de la construction en 1696 par l'empereur Joseph Ier. Certes, ce plan ne fut

Descrizioni

8/9 Veduta del castello di Schönbrunn dalla parte del cortile. Dipinto di Bernardo Bellotto, 1759.

Il pittore veneziano Bernardo Bellotto (1721–1780) aveva studiato presso lo zio Antonio Canal l'arte del paesaggio, quell'arte cioè di rappresentare una città o un paesaggio non solo fotograficamente, ma anche cogliendone il recondito significato.

Come lo zio, prese anch'egli il soprannome di Canaletto e ne seguí le orme; nel 1747, però, lasciò per sempre l'Italia. Operò per quasi due decenni a Dresda e poi, dal 1767 fino alla morte, a Varsavia. Negli anni 1759 e 1760, mentre i Prussiani assediavano e bombardavano la sua seconda patria, Dresda, lavorò a Vienna, soprattutto per conto della corte imperiale. Le vedute dell'epoca, che riguardano la città e i castelli, mostrano piazze, zone a verde ed edifici costruiti nella seconda metà del secolo testè trascorso. Bellotto fissò col suo pennello la „Vienna moderna", quella del 1760; e Schönbrunn non poteva mancare.

L'artista ha dipinto il grande cortile d'onore, affollato di gente. I suoi personaggi, benchè non ritratti dal vero, sono di grande realismo, tipici della vita che si svolge in una piazza. Qui comunque egli fissò un episodio storico che aveva entusiasmato la Vienna dell'epoca: il 12 agosto 1759 il luogotenente maresciallo di campo Laudon aveva ottenuto una grande vittoria su Federico II di Prussia vicino a Kunersdorf, ad est dell'Oder. Nel diario di Khevenhüller si può leggere quanto segue: „Il 16 (agosto) le Loro maestà si recarono alle 10,30 al convento degli Agostiniani, sulla Landstrasse, in occasione della festa di S. Rocco. Sulla via del ritorno li raggiunse, a cavallo, accompagnato da venti trombettieri e da quattro maestri di posta, il tenente colonnello Giuseppe Kinski, che portò la notizia della vittoria del generale Laudon."

Il quadro si trova nel Museo di storia dell'arte.

12/13 Johann Bernhard Fischer von Erlach, progetti per il castello imperiale di Schönbrunn, circa 1693 e 1696.

Giovanni Bernardo Fischer von Erlach (1656–1723), il „grande Vecchio" dell'architettura tedesca, pubblicò nel 1721 un volume con grandi incisioni su rame che intitolò „Progetto per un'architettura storica".

In quest'opera Fischer esamina i problemi relativi all'architettura a partire dall'antichità, con ricostruzioni dei primi grandi edifici dell'umanità. Alle fine presenta anche le proprie opere.

Tra queste si trova il primo progetto, non realizzato, di Schönbrunn, chiamato, in una didascalia, „Venérie Imperiale", cioè castello di caccia imperiale.

In primo piano è visibile un grande spiazzo che avrebbe dovuto essere adibito a feste e a tornei, con una tenda per l'Imperatore e i suoi ospiti; lo spiazzo è delimitato dal grande portone ornato da colonne. Su queste poggiano delle aquile, le stesse che oggi adornano gli obelischi, ai lati del portone.

Il secondo progetto fantasioso, anzi fantastico, si realizza. Fischer von Erlach trasferisce il castello dalla collina al piano. Nella veduta del cortile d'onore così come nella planimetria sono riconoscibili i particolari del progetto che fu poi accettato dall'Imperatore Giu-

Projekt der Realität. Im wahrsten Sinne des Wortes hat Fischer von Erlach das Schloß von der Höhe heruntergeholt. Die Ansicht der Ehrenhofseite und der ebenfalls publizierte Grundriß (Seite 39) lassen alle Einzelheiten des Planes erkennen, der 1696 von Kaiser Joseph I., damals noch Römischer König, als Grundlage des Baues akzeptiert wurde. Zwar wurde auch dieser Plan nur teilweise in der ersten Bauphase bis um 1700 verwirklicht und unter Maria Theresia wesentlich verändert, aber die Anordnung der Baublöcke, die Anlage des Ehrenhofes, sogar der Standort der Gloriette sind schon von Fischer von Erlach bestimmt worden.

15   Die Gartenfassade des Schlosses.

Die heutige Gestalt der Gartenfassade geht auf die Erneuerung des Daches und der Balustraden sowie auf die Vereinfachung und Begradigung der Fassade im klassizistischen Geschmack nach Plänen des Architekten Johann Aman zurück. Seine nicht sehr gelungenen Veränderungen aus den Jahren 1817–1819 sind besonders an der Gartenseite bemerkbar, was bei einem Vergleich des heutigen Zustands mit dem Gemälde Bellottos (Seite 67) deutlich wird. Besonders auffällig ist die strenge Führung des kantigen Hauptgesimses, das im Gegensatz zu den von Pacassi hoch angelegten Rundungen steht, die eine Steigerung der Fassade zur Mitte hin bewirkten. Dennoch strahlt die Gartenfassade weltweite Macht und fröhliche Gelassenheit, zugleich Intimität und Urbanität aus.
In der Mitte erhebt sich der Baukörper über die Höhe des übrigen Gebäudes in Gestalt eines sogenannten Belvederes. Es wird auf der Gartenseite seit etwa 1819 von Doppeladler und Kriegstrophäen bekrönt, Symbol des siegreichen Kaisertums. Darunter befindet sich die sogenannte Vogeluhr, die anstelle einer älteren runden Uhr hier eingebaut wurde.

16   Brunnengruppe im Ehrenhof von Johann B. Hagenauer.

Springbrunnen plante schon Fischer von Erlach in beiden Hälften des Ehrenhofes, und auf Bellottos Hofansicht erkennen wir sie deutlich. Jeder der beiden ist mit einer vielfigurigen Gruppe geschmückt. Unter Maria Theresia mußten diese barocken Skulpturen kleineren, klassizistischen weichen, die dem Wasser größeren Raum gewährten, Johann Baptist Hagenauer schuf die linke der beiden, eine Allegorie der 1722 bei der Teilung Polens gegründeten Königreiche Galizien und Lodomerien und des Großfürstentums Siebenbürgen.

25   Gobelinsalon: Allegorische Darstellung der zwölf Monate auf den Sitzpolstern und Rückenlehnen der Fauteuils.

Die Sitzpolster und Rückenlehnen der sechs Fauteuils des „Gobelinsalons" sind mit kleinen Tapisserien bezogen und stellen in reizvollen Genreszenen die zwölf Monate dar. Die Entwürfe für alle diese großen und kleinen Szenen wurden nach Gemälden des niederländischen Malers David Teniers d. J. (1610–1690) angefertigt, dessen manchmal derbe, aber immer treffende und lebensvolle Darstellungen des Volkslebens in jeder großen Gemäldegalerie anzutreffen sind.
Wandteppiche fehlten in keinem europäischen Fürstenschloß des

Emperor Joseph I – at that time still King of Rome – as a basis for construction. In fact, this design was only partially carried out during the first phase of construction up to 1700 and substantially modified during the reign of Maria Theresa, but the layout of the building units and the parade-ground as well as the location of the Gloriette were determined by Fischer von Erlach.

15   The garden façade of the palace.

The present form of the south façade can be traced not only to the renovation of the roof and balustrades, but also to the simplifying of the façade in the style of classicism. The illconceived modifications, carried out to the designs of Johann Aman from 1817 to 1819, are especially noticeable on the side facing the garden. This becomes even more apparent when the present form is compared to that depicted in Bellotto's painting (page 67). Particularly striking is the severity of the square-edged cornice in contrast to Pacassi's rounded edges, which had shifted emphasis toward the middle of the façade. Nevertheless the garden façade manages to project an aura of global power and cheerful composure, blending intimacy and urbanity.
In the middle the so-called belvedere, or balcony, rises above the level of the rest of the building. Since about 1819 it has been crowned by a two-headed eagle and war trophies to symbolize the glorious empire. Underneath a clock that shows time horizontally, the so-called "Vogelclock", can be found in place of the former circular clock.

16   Fountain statuary by Johann B. Hagenauer in the Great Court of Schönbrunn.

Fountains were designed by Fischer von Erlach for both halves of the so-called „Great Court", which can be recognized in Bellotto's courtyard veduta. They are adorned with a group of figures. Under Maria Theresa the baroque statuary had to make way for a smaller, neoclassical one that alloted more visual space to the water. Johann Baptist Hagenauer created the left group of figures as an allegorical representation of the Kingdoms of Galicia and Lodomeria and the Principality of Transylvania that were created as a result of the division of Poland in 1772.

25   The "Gobelin" Drawing-Room: Allegorical representations of the twelve months of the year on the tapestries covering the seats and the backs of the arm-chairs.

The tapestries used for the seat cushions and backs of the six armchairs of the "Gobelin" Drawing-Room represent the twelve months of the year by way of charming genre scenes. The designs of all the large and small scenes are copied from the paintings of the Dutch artist, David Teniers d. J. (1610–1690), whose occasionally coarse but always accurate and lively depictions of peasant life can be found in any large art gallery.
Tapestries were among the furnishings of every European palace during the Baroque. They are a legacy of the Renaissance, during which period they had already become indispensable requisites of princely life.

réalisé qu'en partie et subit ensuite des modifications sensibles sous Marie-Thérèse mais l'ordonnancement des bâtiments, le plan de la cour d'Honneur, même l'emplacement de la Gloriette ont déjà été fixés par Fischer von Erlach.

15 *La façade du château sur les jardins.*

L'aspect actuel de la façade vient de ce que le toit et les balustrades ont été refaits et la façade ellememe dépouillée et rectifiée selon les plans de l'architecte Johann Aman. Les remaniements effectués de 1817 à 1819 et qui témoignent de son peu de talent sont particulièrement perceptibles du côté jardin; on le voit dans le tableau de Bellotto (page 67). Ce qui frappe surtout, c'est la ligne sévère de la corniche principale à arête vive qui s'oppose aux parties supérieures rondes de Pacassi qui faissaient ressortir la partie centrale. Cependant, de la façade sur les jardins du château émane un air de puissance mondiale et de tranquillité joyeuse ainsi que d'intimité et d'urbanité.
L'avant-corps central est plus haut que le reste du bâtiment et forme ce qu'on appelle un belvédère. Depuis 1819, il est couronné du côté jardin par un aigle à deux têtes et de trophées guerriers, symboles d'un empire victorieux. Il-surmonte une horloge à cadran horizontal (Vogeluhr) qui a remplacé une ancienne horloge ronde.

16 *Sculptures du bassin de la cour d'honneur de Johann B. Hagenauer.*

Fischer von Erlach avait projeté des fontaines dans les deux parties de la cour d'Honneur comme on peut le voir distinctement sur la vue de la cour de Bellotto; elles sont chacune décorée d'un groupe de plusieurs statues. Sous Marie-Thérèse, ces sculptures baroques durent céder la place à d'autres, plus petites, de style néo-classique. Celles de gauche, exécutées par Johann Baptist Hagenauer sont une allégorie des royaumes de Galicie et de Lodomérie, fondés en 1772 après le partage de la Pologne et de la principauté de Transylvanie.

25 *Le salon des tapisseries: Les sièges et les dossiers des six fauteuils représentent les douze mois de l'année.*

Les sièges et les dossiers des six fauteuils du „Salon des Gobelins" – de petites tapisseries – représentent les douze mois de l'année dans des charmantes scènes de genre. Les cartons pour toutes ces grandes et petites scènes ont été exécutés d'après des tableaux du peintre néerlandais David Téniers le jeune (1610–1690), dont on peut voir dans chaque grande galerie de peintures les représentations parfois grossières mais toujours frappantes de vérité et vivantes de la vie populaire.
Les tapisseries ne manquaient dans aucun château princier européen de l'époque baroque. Les manufactures hollandaises des 16 ème et 17 ème siècles comptaient au nombre des plus importantes; ce ne fut que dans la deuxième moitié du 17 ème siècle avec la fondation de la manufacture des Gobelins à Paris que les productions françaises gagnèrent également en importance, par la suite – et jusqu'à maintenant – on nomme souvent faussement „Gobelins" toutes les tapisseries, également celles qui sont suspendues dans la grande salle du côté est du château de Schönbrunn depuis 1873. En réalité, il s'agit

seppe I, allora ancora re dell'Impero romano. Ciò è testimoniato anche dalla relativa didascalia. Questo progetto, a dire il vero, fu realizzato solo in parte, fino circa all'anno 1700. Sotto Maria Teresa esso fu modificato, ma, per la posizione delle varie costruzioni del cortile d'onore e persino della Gloriette, si tenne presente il progetto originario di Fischer von Erlach.

15 *La facciata del castello che dà sul giardino.*

L'attuale facciata che dà sul giardino è il risultato di lavori di rinnovo del tetto e delle balaustrate, nonchè della rielaborazione della facciata, di gusto classicheggiante, secondo i disegni dell'architetto Giovanni Aman. Le modifiche apportate da questo architetto negli anni 1817-1819 sono spesso discutibili e sono visibili soprattutto nella parte che dà sul giardino. Ce ne rendiamo conto se confrontiamo lo stato attuale della facciata con il dipinto di Bellotto (pag. 67) che raffigura invece la facciata precedente. Colpisce particolarmente il cornicione principale, a spigolo vivo, così severo nella sua realizzazione; esso contrasta con le decorazioni, arrontondate, del Pacassi, che danno slancio alla facciata nella parte mediana.
Nel mezzo dell'edificio si innalza un ulteriore corpo a formare un belvedere. Dalla parte che dà sul giardino esso è decorato, dal 1819, con un'aquila bicipite e con dei trofei di guerra, simboli del glorioso impero. Al di sotto di questi è collocata la cosiddetta „Vogeluhr" (orologio) che ha sostituito un vecchio orologio rotondo.

16 *Gruppo scultoreo nella fontana del cortile d'onore di Johann B. Hagenauer.*

Già Fischer von Erlach aveva inserito, in entrambe le parti del cortile d'onore, due fontane a zampillo che si possono chiaramente individuare anche nella veduta del cortile dipinta da Bellotto. Le fontane sono ornate con gruppi scultorei.
All'epoca di Maria Teresa queste possenti figure barocche furono sostituite da altre, più piccole e di stile classicheggiante, in quanto si voleva dare maggior spazio ai giochi d'acqua. A Giovanni B. Hagenauer si deve il gruppo scultoreo di sinistra, un'allegoria dei regni di Galizia, di Lodomeria e del Principato di Transilvania, fondati nel 1772, in seguito alla divisione della Polonia.

25 *Salone degli arazzi: I sedili e le spalliere delle sei poltrone.*

I sedili e le spalliere delle sei poltrone che si trovano nel salone dei Gobelins sono coperti da piccoli arazzi, che rappresentano, con deliziose scene, i dodici mesi dell'anno. Modelli per tutte queste scene furono i dipinti del pittore fiammingo Davide Teniers, il Giovane (1610-1690): di lui si trovano, nelle maggiori pinacoteche, rappresentazioni vivaci e fedeli della vita del popolo.
Gli arazzi sono presenti in tutti i palazzi principeschi del Barocco. Sono l'eredità del Rinascimento che considerava i tappeti tessuti una decorazione, variabile delle pareti; erano ritenuti requisiti indispensabili di una corte principesca.
Nel XVI e XVII secolo importantissimi erano gli arazzi di provenienza fiamminga; solo nella seconda metà del XVII secolo acquistarono importanza anche i prodotti francesi grazie all'apertura della fabbrica

Barock. Auch sie sind Erbstücke der Renaissance, die den gewirkten Teppich bereits als variablen Wandbehang, als unentbehrliches Requisit fürstlicher Hofhaltung kannte. Zu den wichtigsten Manufakturen des 16. und 17. Jahrhunderts zählten die niederländischen; erst in der zweiten Hälfte des 17. Jahrhunderts gewannen mit der Gründung der Gobelin-Manufaktur in Paris auch die französischen Erzeugnisse Bedeutung. In der Folge – und bis zum heutigen Tag – werden oftmals alle Wandteppiche fälschlich „Gobelins" genannt, so auch jene, die in dem großen Saal an der Ostseite Schönbrunns seit 1873 aufgespannt sind. Tatsächlich handelt es sich hier, ebenso wie im Napoleonzimmer, um Brüsseler Tapisserien des 18. Jahrhunderts.

26 Theateraufführungen in Schönbrunn mit Kindern Maria Theresias in verschiedenen Rollen. Gemälde aus der Schule Martin van Meytens.

Die habsburgischen Herrscher des Barock liebten Musik und Theater nicht nur als Zuhörer, sondern auch als Mitwirkende. Maria Theresia erzog ihre Kinder in dieser Tradition. Die vielen Familienfeste, vor allem die in Wien besonders gefeierten Namenstage, gaben Gelegenheit, vor einem ausgewählten Publikum aufzutreten. Solange die Kinder klein waren, wurden oft als Überraschung für Vater oder Mutter italienische oder französische Komödien, Ballette oder Schäferspiele aufgeführt, wobei der andere Elternteil die Kinder anleitete: viel Dressur, aber auch viel echte Fröhlichkeit! Von den halbwüchsigen oder erwachsenen Erzherzoginnen konnten schon kleine italienische Opern, sogenannte Operetten, einstudiert werden. Ein prominenter Anlaß zu einem solch anspruchsvollen Unterfangen war die Hochzeit Josephs II. mit Maria Josepha von Bayern im Januar 1765. Trotz der kalten Jahreszeit begab man sich nach Schönbrunn und spielte im Zeremoniensaal Christoph Willibald Glucks eigens für diesen Anlaß zu einem Text von Metastasio komponierte Operette „Il parnasso confuso". Die Erzherzogin Maria Amalie trat als Apollo auf, drei ihrer Schwestern spielten Musen, Erzherzog Peter Leopold dirigierte vom Cembalo aus.
Am nächsten Abend wurde von Berufssängern die Serenade „Il trionfo d'amore" von Gaßmann aufgeführt, mit einer Balletteinlage, die von den jüngsten Geschwistern des kaiserlichen Bräutigams getanzt wurde: von der neunjährigen Maria Antoinette als „Flore" und ihren Brüdern Ferdinand Karl und Maximilian Franz, die ein Jahr älter bzw. ein Jahr jünger waren.

27 Theateraufführung anläßlich der Vermählung Josephs II. mit Isabella von Parma, 1760. Gemälde von Martin van Meytens. (Zeremoniensaal.)

Dargestellt ist hier das Publikum. Links und rechts von Kaiser Franz Stephan und Kaiserin Maria Theresia füllen die erste Reihe die Kinder, die hier den Darbietungen von Berufsschauspielern und Berufsmusikern beiwohnen. Anlaß zu diesem Theaterabend im Redoutensaal der Hofburg ist das Fest der Vermählung des zukünftigen Königs und Kaisers Joseph II. mit der schönen bourbonischen Prinzessin Isabella von Parma. Das Hochzeitspaar sitzt zu Seiten des Kaiserpaars.
Auch für das Schönbrunner Schloßtheater wurden selbstverständlich Berufsschauspieler engagiert, meist italienische oder französische, seit Joseph II. (1765 bzw. 1780–1790) auch deutsche Truppen. Eine be-

In the sixteenth and seventeenth centuries the Dutch were among the most important manufacturers; French products did not achieve prominence until the establishment of the famous tapestry works by Gobelin in Paris. Since then – and up to the present day – tapestries (such as these, hung in the Great Hall in the east wing of the palace in 1873) have often falsely been referred to as "gobelins". Actually, the tapestries here, like those in the Napoleon Room, are Brussels tapestries from the eighteenth century.

26 Theatre performances at Schönbrunn, with Maria Theresa's children in various roles. Painting by the School of Martin van Meytens.

The Hapsburg rulers of the Baroque were not only passive recipients, but also active participants in matters of music and theatre. Maria Theresa raised her children in this tradition. Performances before a selected audience were occasioned by numerous family celebrations, especially for the nameday festivities so popular in Vienna. One of the parents would assist and direct the young children in surprising the other parent with a rendition of Italian or French comedies, ballets, or pastoral plays: plenty of arduous training, but spiced with genuine gaiety! Small Italian operas, called operettes, were performed by the adolescent or post-adolescent archduchesses. An occasion for one such demanding enterprise was the marriage of Joseph II to Maria Josepha of Bavaria in January 1765. Despite the season the nuptial festivities took place in the Ceremonial Hall of Schönbrunn, where, to the lyrics of Metastasio, an operette composed by Gluck especially for the occasion was performed: "Il parnasso confuso". The Archduchess Maria Amalie appeared in the role of Apollo, three of her sisters played Muses, and the Archduke Peter Leopold played the harpsichord and conducted.
On the next evening Gassmann's serenade, "Il trionfo d'amore", was sung by professionals, with a ballet interlude danced by the imperial groom's youngest brothers and sisters: with the nine year-old Marie Antoinette as "Flore", joined by her brothers Ferdinand Karl and Maximilian Franz, who were ten and eight years old at the time.

27 A theatre performance on the occasion of the marriage of Joseph II to Isabella of Parma, 1760. Painting by Martin van Meytens. (Ceremonial Hall.)

It is the audience which is depicted here. In the first row we see Emperor Francis and Empress Maria Theresa with their children on either side, watching the performance of professional actors and musicians. The occasion for this theatre performance at the Ballroom (Redoutensal) of the Hofburg was the wedding of the future King and Emperor Joseph II to the beautiful Bourbon princess Isabella of Parma. The bride and groom are seated next to the imperial couple. At the palace theatre of Schönbrunn, too, professional actors were employed, with German performers joining their French and Italian counterparts only during the reign of Joseph II (1765, 1780–1790). The theatre flourished especially during Napoleon's sojourns in 1805 and 1809. The French emperor attended the performances regularly, surrounded by his General Staff in their lavish uniforms and golden epaulets. In 1805 he commissioned Cherubini to perform a concert, and in 1809 he ordered Mozart's Don Giovanni and Racine's Phaedra (in Schiller's German translation) to be performed. Not any less

ici, comme dans la chambre de Napoléon, de tapisseries de Bruxelles du 18ème siècle.

26 Représentations théâtrales à Schönbrunn avec des enfants de Marie-Thérèse dans différents rôles. Tableau de l'Ecole de Martin van Meytens.

Les souverains Habsbourg de l'époque baroque aimaient non seulement à écouter de la musique et des pièces de théâtre mais également à en jouer. Marie-Thérèse éleva ses enfants dans cette tradition. Les nombreuses fêtes de famille surtout les fêtes qui étaient célébrées particulièrement à Vienne donnaient l'occasion de se produire devant un public choisi. Aussi longtemps que les enfants furent petits, on représenta souvent comme surprise pour le père ou la mère (l'un des parents dirigeant les enfants) des comédies italiennes ou françaises, des ballets ou des bergeries. Une occasion éminente pour une entreprise si exigeante fut le mariage de Joseph II avec Marie-Josèphe de Bavière en janvier 1765. En dépit de la saison froide, on se rendit à Schönbrunn et on joua dans la salle des Cérémonies une opérette composée exprès à cette occasion par Gluck sur un texte de Métastase „Il parnasso confuso". L'archiduchesse Marie-Amélie se produisit en tant qu'Apollon, ses trois sœurs jouèrent les Muses, l'archiduc Pierre-Leopold dirigea la représentation tout en jouant lui-même le violoncelle.
Le soir suivant, des chanteurs professionnels donnèrent la sérénade de Gassmann „Il trionfo d'amore" avec un intermède de ballet qui fut dansé par les quatre plus jeunes frères et sœurs de l'époux impérial: Marie-Antoinette, âgée de neuf ans, dans „Flore" et ses frères Ferdinand-Charles et Maximilien-François respectivement d'un an plus âgé ou plus jeune.

27 Représentation théâtrale a l'occasion du mariage de Joseph II avec Isabelle de Parme, 1760. Peinture de Martin van Meytens. (Salle des cérémonies.)

C'est le public qui est représenté ici. Au premier rang, à droite et à gauche de l'empereur François Etienne et de l'impératrice Marie-Thérèse, sont assis les enfants qui assistent ici à la représentation donnée par des acteurs et des musiciens professionnels. Cette soirée théâtrale à la Redoutensaal de la Hofburg a eu lieu à l'occasion de la fête du mariage du futur empereur et roi Joseph II avec la belle princesse de Bourbon, Isabelle de Parme. Les mariés sont assis de part et d'autre du couple impérial.
Pour le théâtre du château de Schönbrunn, on engageait aussi naturellement des chanteurs professionnels, la plupart du temps italiens ou français mais également des compagnies allemandes depuis Joseph II (1765 ou 1780-1790). Le théâtre du château de Schönbrunn vécut une période particulièrement faste pendant les séjours de Napoléon en 1805 et 1809. L'empereur des Français se rendait très souvent aux représentations entourés de généraux aux uniformes chamarrés d'or. En 1805, il appela Cherubini pour donner un concert, en 1809, ordonna entre autres la représentation du Don Giovanni de Mozart et de la Phèdre de Racine dans la version allemande de Schiller.
Les représentations théâtrales données pendant le congrès de Vienne (1814-1815) devant un public international ne furent pas moins nombreuses mais sûrement encore plus insouciantes. Le théâtre du

Gobelin a Parigi. Ancor oggi gli arazzi vengono spesso erroneamente chiamati „Gobelins"; è il caso di quelli che sono esposti sin dal 1873 nella grande sala dell'ala est di Schönbrunn. Si tratta, e ciò vale anche per la stanza di Napoleone, di arazzi provenienti da Bruxelles (XVIII secolo).

26 Rappresentazioni teatrali a Schönbrunn con alcuni figli di Maria Teresa in ruoli diversi. Dipinti della scuola di Martin van Meytens.

Gli Asburgo, all'epoca barocca, amavano la musica e il teatro e lo vivevano non in modo passivo ma attivo. Maria Teresa, nell'educazione dei propri figli, non dimenticò mai questa tradizione. Le feste di famiglia non mancavano: soprattutto in occasione degli onomastici, i ragazzi recitavano di fronte ad un pubblico scelto. Finchè erano piccoli, questi facevano delle sorprese ai genitori: il padre o la madre istruivano i bambini a rappresentare commedie italiane o francesi, balletti o scene pastorali. Ciò procurava molto lavoro, ma, alla fine, era un vero e proprio divertimento. Le Arciduchesse, adolescenti o adulte, erano in gardo di esibirsi in piccole opere italiane, dette operette. Un'occasione del tutto particolare fu il matrimonio di Giuseppe II con Giuseppina di Bavaria, nel gennaio del 1765.
Nonostante la stagione fredda, la famiglia imperiale si recò al gran completo a Schönbrunn, dove ebbe luogo, nella sala delle cerimonie, la rappresentazione dell'operetta „Il parnasso confuso", che Gluck aveva scritto per quest'occasione su un testo di Metastasio. L'Arciduchessa Maria Amalia impersonava Apollo, tre delle sorelle le muse, mentre l'Arciduca Pietro Leopoldo dirigeva, suonando contemporaneamente il clavicembalo.
Le sera seguente dei cantanti professionisti presentarono la serenata „Il trionfo d'amore" di Gaßmann, mentre il corpo di ballo era costituito dai fratellini dello sposo, e cioè da Maria Antonietta, che allora aveva nove anni, nella parte di „Flore", dai fratelli Ferdinando Carlo, di dieci anni, e Massimiliano Francesco, di otto anni.

27 Rappresentazione teatrale in occasione delle nozze di Giuseppe II con Isabella di Parma, 1760. Dipinto di Martin van Meytens. (Sala delle cerimonie.)

Qui viene rappresentato il pubblico. In prima fila, a sinistra e a destra dell'Imperatore Francesco Stefano e dell'Imperatrice Maria Teresa, sono raffigurati i loro figli, che seguono le rappresentazioni di attori e musicisti professionisti. Questa serata musicale fu organizzata nella Redoutensaal dela Hofburg in occasione delle nozze del futuro Re ed Imperatore Giuseppe II con la bella Principessa borbonica, Isabella di Parma. La coppia di sposi è seduta accanto alla coppia imperiale.
Per il teatro del castello si ingaggiavano solitamente degli attori professionisti, per lo più italiani o francesi. Con Giuseppe II (1765 e 1780-1790) furono chiamate anche delle compagnie teatrali tedesche. Durante la permanenza a Vienna di Napoleone nel 1805 e nel 1809 il teatro di Schönbrunn ebbe una particolare fioritura.
L'Imperatore dei Francesi presenziò molto spesso alle rappresentazioni teatrali, circondato dai generali nelle loro divise sfavillanti d'oro. Nel 1805 Napoleone chiamò Cherubini a tenere un concerto, nel 1809 fece rappresentare il „Don Giovanni" di Mozart e la „Fedra" di Racine nella versione tedesca di Schiller.

sondere Blüte erlebte das Schönbrunner Schloßtheater während der Aufenthalte Napoleons in den Jahren 1805 und 1809. Der Kaiser der Franzosen besuchte sehr häufig die Vorstellungen, umgeben von der Generalität in goldstrotzenden Uniformen. Er berief 1805 Cherubini zu einem Konzert, befahl 1809 unter anderem die Aufführung von Mozarts Don Giovanni und von Racines Phaedra in der deutschen Fassung Schillers. Nicht weniger häufig, sicher aber noch unbeschwerter waren die Theateraufführungen, die während des Wiener Kongresses (1814/15) vor einer internationalen Gesellschaft gespielt wurden.

Das Schloßtheater wurde nach Plänen Pacassis gebaut und 1747 eröffnet, von Hohenberg um 1766/67 im Stil des späten Rokoko dekoriert. Durch Erneuerungen und durch die Adaptierung für das Reinhardt-Seminar 1924 wurden Innenraum und Bühne seither wiederholt verändert. Jahrelang spielte im Sommer die Wiener Kammeroper in Schönbrunn und zauberte Festspielatmosphäre in dieses älteste Theater Wiens.

28/29 Rösselzimmer: Das große Jagdbild von Philipp Ferdinand von Hamilton und vier Pferdeporträts: Hermoso, Excellente, General, Philosopho.

Im aristokratischen Leben der Barockzeit spielte das edle Pferd eine wichtige Rolle. Der kaiserliche Oberststallmeister und sein Amt verwalteten den Marstall – in Schönbrunn waren allein Stallungen für 400 Pferde vorgesehen –, die Gestüte und die Reitschulen, von denen die „Spanische" als einzigartige Institution noch heute besteht. Auch die Leib-, Gala-, Stadt-, Kutschier-, Jagd- und Reisewagen sowie die Hundemeuten unterstanden ihm und wurden von einem großen Personal betreut. Letztlich war er auch für den Ablauf der großen zeremoniellen Wagen- und Schlittenfahrten verantwortlich. Die schönsten und besten Pferde wurden „porträtiert" und Gestüts- oder Pferdegalerien angelegt. Künstler, die sich als Pferde- und Hundemaler spezialisiert hatten, wie die niederländischen Brüder Hamilton, lebten als „Hoftiermaler" ausschließlich dieser Aufgabe. Porträts der Hofgesellschaft oder Darstellungen der Landschaft waren Sache anderer Spezialisten.

Die Bilder der vier Pferde – Hermoso, Excellente, General, Philosopho – wurden von Johann Georg Hamilton (1672–1737) um 1725 gemalt und später von Johann Christian Brand (1722–1795) mit einem Landschaftshintergrund versehen. Der Rappe Hermoso, das „Favorit-Reitpferd" Kaiser Karls VI., wird zu einem Prunksattel geführt; General, ein geapfelter Dunkelbrauner in der Piaffe, ist gemeinsam mit einem Reitknecht abgebildet, auf dessen Schulter eine Handdecke mit dem in Gold gestickten Monogramm Kaiser Karls VI. liegt; der Rappe Excellente und der Schimmel Philosopho posieren dem Maler in der Levade.

Die an der „Parforcejagd Kaiser Josephs I. in den Marchauen" beteiligten Damen der Hofgesellschaft kutschieren in graziöser Weise ihre zierlichen und eleganten zweirädrigen Cabriolets selbst – da es über Stock und Stein geht, eine Aufgabe, die einige Geschicklichkeit erforderte. Das Bild entstand um 1730, sein Urheber ist Philipp Ferdinand von Hamilton (1664–1750), vollendet wurde es durch Martin Rausch von Traubenberg im Jahr 1752.

frequent and even more carefree were the plays performed for an international audience during the Congress of Vienna (1814–15).

The palace theatre was built to a design by Pacassi and opened in 1747, then re-decorated in late rococo by Hohenberg in 1766/67. Since then the stage and interior have been modified repeatedly for both renovation and the adaption of the theatre to the needs of the Max Reinhardt School of Dramatic Art in 1924. For many years, the "Wiener Kammeroper" performed in Schönbrunn every summer and conjured up an atmosphere of music festivals in this oldest theater of Vienna.

28/29 Room of the Horses: The large painting of a hunting scene by Philipp Ferdinand von Hamilton, and four of the horse portraits: Hermoso, Excellente, General, Philosopho.

The horse played an important role in the lives of baroque aristocrats. At Schönbrunn the outbuildings contained stables for more than four hundred horses. The Master of the Horse and other imperial equerries administered, in addition to the stables, the stud-farms and the riding schools, of which the "Spanish" Riding School still exists. He was also in charge of all the imperial coaches and carriages as well as the hounds and the large staff looking after them. It was his task to organise the grand ceremonial carriage and sleigh rides.

The best and most beautiful of the horses were "portrayed" and arranged in horse galleries. Artists who had specialized in the painting of horses and dogs, such as the Dutch brothers Hamilton, limited themselves exclusively to their chosen genre as "Painter of Animals to the Court". Portraits of courtly society or of landscapes were the domains of other artists.

The portraits of the four horses Hermoso, Excellente, General, and Philosopho were rendered by Johann Georg Hamilton (1672–1737) in 1725, with the backgrounds being furnished by the landscape painter Johann Christian Brand (1722–1795). The black Hermoso, the "favourite riding horse" of Emperor Charles VI, is being led to a dress saddle; the dark brown, dappled General is portrayed in the piaffe next to a groom shouldering a saddle-cloth with the golden brocade monogram of Charles VI; the black Excellente and the white Philosopho are depicted in the levade.

The ladies of the court participating in the "Coursing of Emperor Joseph I in the marshes of the River March" are shown driving their elegant little two-wheeled cabriolets themselves. The driving up hill and down dale required a good deal of skill. The painting was begun in 1730 by Philipp Ferdinand von Hamilton (1664–1750) and completed by Martin Rausch von Traubenberg in 1752.

Gartenparterre: Die trauernde Artemisia von Johann B. Hagenauer – der Volksmund nennt sie „Maria Theresia".
Garden parterre: Artemisia mourning the death of her husband – popularly called "Maria Theresa" – by Johann B. Hagenauer.
Parterre du jardin: Artemisia en deuil de Johann B. Hagenauer – elle a été surnommée „Marie-Thérèse" par la vox populi.
Parterre del giardino: L'Artemisia afflitta di Johann B. Hagenauer, che nel linguaggio popolare viene chiamata „Maria Teresa".

94

Doppelstatue Alexanders des Großen und seiner Mutter Olympia von Wilhelm Beyer. – Flötenspielender Merkur von Ignaz Platzer.
Alexander the Great and his mother Olympia, sculpture by Wilhelm Beyer. – Mercury playing the flute by Ignaz Platzer.
Statue double d'Alexandre le Grand et de sa mère Olympia de Wilhelm Beyer. – Mercure jouant de la flûte de Ignaz Platzer.
Statua „doppia" di Alessandro il Grande e di sua madre Olimpia di Wilhelm Beyer. – Mercurio che suona il flauto di Ignaz Platzer.

Obelisk und Neptunbrunnen von Ferdinand von Hohenberg.
Obelisk and the Fountain of Neptune by Ferdinand von Hohenberg.
L'obélisque et la fontaine de Neptune de Ferdinand de Hohenberg.
Obelisco e fontana di Nettuno di Ferdinand von Hohenberg.

Gloriette

château e été construit d'après les plans de Pacassi, inauguré en 1747 et décoré par Hohenberg vers 1766/67 dans le style de la fin du rococo. Pour bien des années l'opéra-bouffe de Vienne jouait à Schönbrunn en été et faisait naître une atmosphère de festival dans ce plus ancien théâtre de Vienne.

28/29 Salon des chevaux: Le grand tableau de chasse de Philippe Ferdinand de Hamilton et quatre portraits de chevaux: Hermoso, Excellente, General, Philosopho.

Dans la vie aristocratique de l'époque baroque, le cheval jouait un rôle important. Le Grand Ecuyer impérial et son service dirigeaient les écuries de Mars – à Schönbrunn, seulement, on avait prévu des écuries pouvant abriter 400 chevaux –, les haras et les manèges dont „l'espagnol", institution unique existe encore de nos jours. Les voitures de même que les meutes de chiens étaient placées sous l'autorité du Grand Ecuyer. Enfin, le Grand Ecuyer était responsable du déroulement des grandes sorties de cérémonie en voiture et en traîneau.

Des „portraits" des chevaux les meilleurs et les plus beaux furent exécutés et des galeries de haras ou de chevaux furent créés. Les artistes qui s'étaient spécialisés dans la peinture des chevaux ou des chiens, comme les frères hollandais Hamilton, n'avaient comme „peintres animaliers de la cour" uniquement que cette tâche. Les portraits des courtisans ou les représentations de paysages étaient l'affaire d'autres spécialistes.

Les portraits des quatre chevaux – Hermoso, Excellente, General, Philosopho – ont été peints par Johann Georg Hamilton (1672–1737) vers 1725 et plus tard, par Johann Christian Brand (1722–1795) qui les a dotés d'un paysage à l'arrière-plan. Le moreau Hermoso, le „cheval favori" de l'empereur Charles VI, est mené vers une salle d'apparat; General, brun foncé pommelé, piaffe et est représenté avec son valet d'écurie qui porte sur l'épaule une couverture avec le monogramme de Charles VI brodé en or; le moreau Excellente et le pommelé Philosopho posent devant le peintre en exécutant une levade.

Les dames de la cour participant à la „chasse à courre de l'empereur Joseph Ier près de Marchegg" conduisent elles-mêmes avec grâce leur cabriolet à deux roues fin et élégant. Comme la chasse passe à travers champs, c'est une tâche qui exige une certaine adresse. Le tableau date de 1730; il a été commencé par Philippe Ferdinand von Hamilton (1664–1750) et terminé par Martin Rausch von Traubenberg en 1752.

30 Les portraits doubles de Schönbrunn.

Marie-Christine et Pierre-Léopold. Martin van Meytens, 1750/51. Salle au balcon.
Pierre-Léopold et Charles-Joseph. Martin van Meytens, 1759/60. Salle au balcon.
Marie-Josèphe et Marie-Antoinette. Pierre Benevault, 1759. Chambre rouge.
Des portraits des membres de la famille impériale se trouvent dans presque chacune des salles du château qui est ouverte à la visite. Lorsqu'on regarde les portraits des enfants, on remarque que ceux-ci sont vêtus tout à fait comme des adultes: les filles sont décolletées, portent un corselet à la taille et des bijoux, les garçons ont les cheveux poudrés et une petite épée. On a parfois du mal à deviner

Il teatro di Schönbrunn fu costruito su progetto di Pacassi e inaugurato nel 1747; le decorazioni, del tardo Rococò, sono opera di Hohenberg, che vi lavorò negli anni 1766/67. La scala e il palcoscenico furono spesso modificati e infine, adattati nel 1924 per il Seminario-Reinhardt.

Per tanti anni d'estate l'Opera da Camera Viennese suonava a Schönbrunn creando un atmosfera incantevole di festa musicale in questo teatro più vecchio di Vienna.

28/29 Stanza dei cavalli: Il grande quadro con scene di caccia di Philipp Ferdinand von Hamilton e quattro ritratti equestri: Hermoso, Excellente, General, Philosopho.

Nella vita artistocratica dell'epoca barocca il nobile cavallo aveva un ruolo assai importante. Il capostalliere imperiale e tutte le persone che lavoravano per lui erano responsabili delle stalle (a Schönbrunn c'era posto per 400 destrieri), delle scuderie, delle scuole di equitazione, tra cui quella „spagnola", che ancora oggi funziona. Di competenza del capostalliere erano anche le carrozze (quelle personali, da città, di gala, coperte, scoperte, da caccia, per i lunghi viaggi) e le mute dei cani. Egli si occupava di tutto questo con l'aiuto però di un numero cospicuo di collaboratori. Era anche responsabile dello svolgimento dei grandi viaggi di protocollo.

I migliori cavalli e anche i più belli venivano „ritratti", i dipinti trovavano posto in apposite gallerie. C'erano degli artisti specializzati nel dipingere cani e cavalli, per esempio i fratelli olandesi Hamilton che vivevano di questo lavoro e avevano il titolo di „pittori di corte per gli animali". Altri specialisti avevano il compito di ritrarre la Corte o di dipingere il paesaggio.

I quadri dei quattro cavalli (Hermoso, Excellente, General e Philosopho) sono opera di Giovanni Giorgio Hamilton (1672–1737), che li dipinse intorno al 1725. Giovanni Cristiano Brand (1722–1795) vi aggiunse, sullo sfondo, un paesaggio. Il morello Hermoso, il cavallo favorito di Carlo VI, è fornito di una splendida sella. Generale, un animale dal mantello marrone scuro in posizione di „Piaffe", invece è immortalato insieme ad uno scudiero sulla cui spalla è posata una coperta col monogramma, ricamato in oro, dell'Imperatore Carlo VI. Il morello Excellente e il cavallo bianco Philosopho posano per il pittore nella „Levade".

Le signore di corte che prendono parte alla „Caccia par force" dell'Imperatore Giuseppe I nei boschi della March, guidano da sole ed modo molte grazioso, le loro eleganti carrozzelle a due ruote. E siccome la strada non era perfettamente piana, le dame, certamente, hanno avuto il loro bel daffare. Il quadro è del 1730, è stato iniziato da Filippo Ferdinando von Hamilton (1664–1750), ma lo ha terminato Martin Rausch von Traubenberg nell'anno 1752.

30 I ritratti „doppi" di Schönbrunn.

Maria Cristina – Pietro Leopoldo. Martin van Meytens, 1750/51. Stanza con balcone.
Pietro Leopoldo – Carlo Giuseppe. Martin van Meytens, 1759/60. Stanza con balcone.
Maria Giuseppina – Maria Antonietta. Pierre Benevault, 1759. Salone rosso.
Si può affermare che in quasi tutte le stanze aperte ai visitatori si trovino dei quadri della famiglia imperiale. Colpisce il fatto che i bambini portino degli abiti da adulti: le ragazze hanno dei corsetti

30 *Schönbrunner Doppelbildnisse.*

Maria Christine – Peter Leopold. Martin van Meytens, 1750/51. Balkonzimmer.
Peter Leopold – Karl Joseph. Martin van Meytens, 1759/60. Balkonzimmer.
Maria Josepha – Marie Antoinette. Pierre Benevault, um 1759. Roter Salon.

Fast in allen Zimmern des Schlosses, die dem Besucher geöffnet sind, befinden sich Bildnisse kaiserlicher Familienmitglieder. An denen der Kinder fällt auf, daß diese ganz in der Art von Erwachsenen gekleidet sind: die Mädchen mit Taillenmiedern, Dekolleté und Schmuck, die Buben mit gepuderten Haaren und Kinderdegen. Ihr Alter ist manchmal kaum zu erkennen. Die Verkleidung entspricht freilich der Realität des Hofzeremoniells.

Das früher entstandene Doppelbildnis zeigt uns den kleinen Kürassier Peter Leopold neben seiner achtjährigen Schwester Maria Christine, die ein Bologneserhündchen auf dem Schoß hält. Auf dem Tisch liegt ein Erzherzogshut, Insigne des Landes und Hauses Österreich.

Karl Joseph und Peter Leopold stehen vor uns als Inhaber ihrer Regimenter. Karl, der zweitgeborene Sohn, war aus politischen Gründen Inhaber eines ungarischen Infanterie-Regiments, Peter Leopold stand bei den Kürassieren, der traditionell vornehmsten Waffengattung. Die beiden Kinder sind etwa 15 und 13 Jahre alt.

In den fünfziger Jahren haben einige wenige französische Maler, darunter Pierre Benevault, etwas vom Pariser Geschmack an den Wiener Hof gebracht: Das Doppelbildnis der Schwestern Maria Josepha und Maria Antoinette um 1759 bemüht sich viel weniger um Porträtähnlichkeit als um die Einkleidung der Mädchen in eine mythologische Thematik oder eine unpersönliche höfische Atmosphäre. Einer „engagierten" Mutter wie Maria Theresia mußten die realistischen Porträts des Meytens mehr zusagen.

Maria Josepha war schon im Alter von etwa acht Jahren nach den Worten ihrer Mutter „ein Opfer der Politik: wenn sie nur ihre Pflicht gegen Gott und ihren Gatten erfüllt ... wäre ich schon zufrieden, selbst wenn sie unglücklich wird." Es sollte anders kommen: Am Tag vor der Vermählung mit dem wenig sympathischen König von Neapel erlag sie den Pocken.

Marie Antoinette (in Wien wurde sie Antonia genannt) wurde 1793 tatsächlich ein Opfer der Politik. Als jüngstes Mädchen – reizvoll und mutwillig zugleich – verwöhnte man sie mehr als die älteren Geschwister. Die leichtlebige Kronprinzessin und junge Königin von Frankreich war an ihrem schweren Schicksal freilich selbst nicht schuldlos.

31 *Kaiser Franz I. und Kaiserin Maria Theresia bei der Gartenarbeit. Tuschzeichnung von Franz Walter.*

32 *Tiergruppen aus dem Schönbrunner Tiergarten von Johann Georg Hamilton, um 1735, vor der Gründung der Menagerie. – Tiere aus Fasangarten und Menagerie von Franz Fuxeder, um 1765.*

Die Worte Dilettant und dilettantisch haben erst heute einen negativen Beiklang. Im 18. Jahrhundert war ein Großteil von dem, was wir heute Wissenschaft nennen, noch in Händen von Dilettanten. Insbesondere fürstliche Personen haben durch ihre Liebhabereien auf naturwissenschaftlichem oder technischem Gebiet entscheidende

30 *Schönbrunn double-portraits.*

Maria Christine – Peter Leopold. Martin van Meytens, 1750/51. Balcony Room.
Peter Leopold – Karl Joseph. Martin van Meytens, 1759/60. Balcony Room.
Maria Josepha – Marie Antoinette. Pierre Benevault, c. 1759. Red Drawing-Room.

Portraits of the imperial family hang in almost every room of the palace open to visitors. Regarding the portraits of the children, it is striking how they are dressed in the manner of adults: the girls in bodices, décolletés, and jewelry, the boys with powdered hair and small sabres. Sometimes it is almost impossible to tell their age. The costumes correspond, of course, to the reality of court ceremony.

The earlier double-portrait depicts the young cuirassier Peter Leopold next to his eight year-old sister, Maria Christine, shown holding a Maltese dog. On the table are the insignia of the crownland of Austria, an archducal coronet.

The Archdukes Karl Joseph and Peter Leopold are posed before us in the uniforms of their own respective regiments. Karl, the second-born son, commanded – out of political considerations! – a Hungarian infantry regiment; Peter Lepold was a cuirassier, traditionally the noblest branch of service. The children are about fifteen and thirteen years of age.

During the fifties a small number of French painters, among them Pierre Benevault, succeeded in introducing something of Parisian taste to the Vienna Court: the double-portrait of the sisters Maria Josepha and Maria Antoinette from 1759 concerns itself less with verisimilitude than with enveloping the girls in a mythological aura or in the impersonal atmosphere of the court. A "devoted" mother such as Maria Theresa preferred Meytens' more naturalistic portraits. According to her mother, Maria Josepha had already become, at the tender age of eight years, "a victim of politics: if she can only fulfill her duties both to God and to her husband, I shall be satisfied, even if she is unhappy". Things turned out differently: on the day preceding her marriage to the rather unappealing King of Naples, she succumbed to smallpox.

Marie Antoinette (in Vienna she was called Antonia) actually did become a victim of politics in 1793. As the youngest of Maria Theresa's daughters – equally charming and mischievous – she was overindulged in comparison to her sisters. The harsh fate suffered by the frivolous Crown Princess and young Queen of France was partly her own fault.

31 *Emperor Francis I and Empress Maria Theresa working in the garden. Ink drawing by Franz Walter.*

32 *Groups of animals from the deer-park at Schönbrunn by Johann Georg Hamilton, circa 1735, prior to the establishment of the menagerie. – Animals from the pheasantry and menagerie by Franz Fuxeder, circa 1765.*

The words "dilettante" and "dilettantish" today have pejorative connotations. In the eighteenth century, however, much of what we now term science was in the hands of dilettantes. Princely personages, especially, were able to either make or promote scientific advances thanks to their passions for natural history or technology. Nicolaus Joseph von Jacquin (1727–1817) was the most important scientist in

leur âge. S'ils étaient habillés ainsi, c'est parce que, en réalité, c'était naturellement exigé par l'étiquette de la cour.

Le portrait double peint plus tôt nous montre le petit cuirassier Pierre-Léopold à côté de sa sœur Marie-Christine qui a alors huit ans et qui tient un bichon bolonais sur ses genoux. Sur la table, il y a un chapeau d'archiduc, insigne du pays et de la maison d'Autriche. Charles-Joseph et Pierre-Leopold se tiennent devant nous en tant que propriétaires de leur régiment. Charles, le deuxième des fils, était propriétaire d'un régiment d'infanterie hongrois, Pierre-Léopold, est chez les cuirassiers, l'arme traditionnellement la plus distinguée. Les deux enfants ont environ 15 et 13 ans.

Dans les années cinquante, quelques peintres français dont Pierre Benevault ont apporté un peu du goût parisien à la cour de Vienne: le portrait double des sœurs Maria-Josèphe et Marie-Antoinette, vers 1759, s'efforce bien moin d'attraper la ressemblance que de placer les jeunes filles dans un thème mythologique ou une atmosphère impersonnelle de cour. D'après les paroles de sa mère, Marie-Josèphe était déjà à l'âge de huit ans environ „une victime de la politique: si seulement elle remplit son devoir envers Dieu et son époux ... je serais déjà contente, même si elle est malheureuse." Le destin devait en décider autrement: la veille de son mariage avec le peu sympathique roi de Naples, elle mourut de la variole. Marie-Antoinette (à Vienne, on la nommait Antonia) fut vraiment une victime de la politique en 1793. La plus jeune des filles – charmante et espiègle à la fois – elle fut bien plus gâtée que ses frères et sœurs aînés. Jeune Dauphine insouciante et jeune reine de France, elle fut d'une certaine manière responsable de son terrible destin.

31   L'empereur François Ier et l'impératrice Marie-Thérèse jardinent. Lavis de Franz Walter.

32   Groupes d'animaux du jardin zoologique de Schönbrunn par Johann Georg Hamilton, vers 1735, avant la fondation de la ménagerie. – Animaux du Fasangarten et ménagerie par Franz Fuxeder, vers 1765.

Au 18 éme siècle, les personnages princiers ont contribué, par l'intérêt qu'ils montraient aux sciences naturelles et de la technique, à les faire progresser de manière décisive. Nicolaus Joseph von Jacquin (1727–1817) était, parmi les savants dont s'entoura François Ier, le scientifique le plus éminent. Sa publication sur le jardin botanique de Schönbrunn contient non seulement des descriptions – mais aussi des icones – des représentations d'une beauté et d'une qualité rares qui s'inspirent des propres aquarelles de Jacquin (page 64).

L'empereur François Ier fit montre d'un intérêt tout particulier pour le jardin botanique et la ménagerie. Il entretenait des rapports aussi bien avec les scientifiques qu'avec les jardiniers; il encourageait les voyages d'herboristerie et les expéditions ainsi que les publications scientifiques sur ces sujets. Il fit ses preuves de jardinier „amateur" comme nous le montre un ravissant dessin à la plume de Franz Walter.

Il aimait à conduire lui-même ses invités dans le jardin hollandais et la ménagerie où le pavillon central, un endroit favori du couple impérial, lui permettait, ainsi qu'à ses invités, de jouir d'une belle vue d'ensemble. Le pavillon avait été projeté par Jadot mais fut seulement construit en 1759 d'après un plan de J. F. Blondel, la fresque du plafond a été peinte par Vincenz Fischer. Des peintures à l'huile représentant des animaux de la menagerie sont suspendues dans le

che segnano la vita, ampie scollature e gioielli, mentre i maschi hanno i capelli incipriati e portano la spada. E' spesso difficile definire l'età di queste creature. Gli abiti rispecchiano la moda della corte a quell'epoca.

Il ritratto „doppio" eseguito anteriormente, ci mostra il piccolo corazziere Pietro Leopoldo accanto alla sorellina, Maria Cristina, di otto anni, che tiene in grembo un cagnolino bolognese. Sul tavolo si può osservare un cappello da Arciduca, insegna dell'Austria e della Casa d'Austria.

Carlo Giuseppe e Pietro Leopoldo ci appaiono nelle loro divise di comandanti di reggimento. Carlo, il secondogenito, per ragioni politiche, comandava infatti un reggimento ungherese di fanteria, mentre Pietro Leopoldo era corazziere, l'arma, per tradizione, più ambita. I ragazzi hanno rispettivamente quindici e tredici anni.

Verso la metà del secolo alcuni pittori francesi, tra questi Benevault, introdussero alla corte viennese il gusto parigino. Per esempio, il ritratto di Maria Giuseppina e di Maria Antonietta, oltre che raffigurare le due sorelle, si sforza di inserirle in una tematica o in una atmosfera impersonale, caratteristica della corte. Certamente, ad una madre „impegnata" quale Maria Teresa, piacevano molto di più i ritratti realistici di un Meytens. A detta della madre, la piccola Maria Giuseppina era già all'età di otto anni, una vittima della politica: „Sarei contenta se soltanto la bambina riuscisse a compiere il proprio dovere verso Dio e il marito, a costo anche della sua stessa felicità". Ma la sorte di Maria Cristina fu ben diversa. Proprio il giorno prima del matrimonio con il poco simpatico Re di Napoli, morì di vaiolo. Maria Antonietta, chiamata a Vienna Antonia, fu nel 1793 la vera vittima della politica. Quando era ragazzina, attraente e simpatica, fu più viziata delle altre sorelle. La giovane Regina di Francia, che ebbe una vita così breve, fu in parte lei stessa colpevole del suo tremendo destino.

31   L'Imperatore Francesco I e l'Imperatrice Maria Teresa mentre si occupano di giardinaggio. Disegno in china di Franz Walter.

32   Gruppi di animali del giardino zoologico di Schönbrunn, di Johann Georg Hamilton, intorno al 1735, prima dell'istituzione del serraglio. – Animali della fagianaia e del serraglio di Franz Fuxeder, intorno al 1765.

Le parole „dilettante" e „dilettantistico" hanno acquistato solo ai nostri giorni un significato negativo. Nel XVIII secolo, quella che noi chiamiamo „scienza" era per lo più nelle mani di dilettanti. L'amore per la scienza o per la tecnica da parte di principi e mecenati, fece si che si facessero degli enormi progressi in questi campi e che si raggiungessero risultati insperati. Nicola Giuseppe von Jacquin (1727–1817) era, da un punto di vista scientifico, il più importante studioso all'epoca dell'Imperatore Francesco I. Interessante è il suo lavoro sul giardino botanico di Schönbrunn: „Plantarum rariorum horti Caesarii Schoenbrunnensis descriptiones et icones". Come il titolo stesso dice, esso non contiene solo „descriptiones" (descrizioni), ma anche „icones", disegni di raro splendore e bellezza che hanno come modello alcuni acquerelli dello stesso Jacquin (pag. 64).

L'Imperatore Francesco I aveva un grande interesse per il giardino botanico e per quello zoologico. Era in stretto contatto con gli scienziati e con i giardinieri, finanziava viaggi scientifici e spedizioni, e si „dilettava" a fare il giardiniere, come mostra un delizioso disegno a

Fortschritte erreicht oder gefördert. Nicolaus Joseph von Jacquin (1727–1817) war der wissenschaftlich bedeutendste der Gelehrten, die Kaiser Franz I. in seinen Kreis holte. Seine Publikation über den Schönbrunner Botanischen Garten „Plantarum rariorum horti Caesarii Schoenbrunnensis descriptiones et icones" enthält, wie der Titel sagt, nicht nur descriptiones – Beschreibungen –, sondern auch icones – Abbildungen von seltener Pracht und Schönheit, die auf Jacquins eigene Aquarelle zurückgehen (Seite 64). Kaiser Franz I. wandte dem Botanischen Garten und der Menagerie sein ganz besonderes Interesse zu. Er pflegte Kontakt mit den Wissenschaftlern ebenso wie mit den Gärtnern, förderte Sammelreisen und Expeditionen, sowie wissenschaftliche Publikationen darüber und „dilettierte" als Gärtner, wie die hübsche Tuschzeichnung von Franz Walter zeigt.

Seine Gäste führte der Kaiser gerne selbst in den Holländischen Garten und die Menagerie, wo der Mittelpavillon, ein Lieblingsaufenthalt des Kaiserpaares, ihm und seinen Gästen Gelegenheit gab, die ganze Anlage zu überschauen. Der Pavillon ist schon von Jadot geplant, aber erst 1759 nach einem Entwurf von J. F. Blondel gebaut und von Vincenz Fischer mit einem Deckengemälde geschmückt worden. Im Pavillon hängen Ölbilder von Tieren, die damals in der Menagerie gehalten wurden; sie sollen von Franz Fuxeder stammen. Unvergleichlich eindrucksvoller sind allerdings die 1724 datierten Tierbilder Johann Georg von Hamiltons aus der kaiserlichen Gemäldegalerie, sie könnten zugleich als lebensvolle, exakte Illustrationen eines Tieratlas dienen.

41 Erzherzogin Maria Theresia im Alter von zehn Jahren. Gemälde von Andreas Möller, 1727.

Gäbe es nicht einen 1727 datierten Kupferstich Schmutzers nach diesem Bild, würde man wohl kaum glauben, daß die schöne Erzherzogin im dunkelblauen Atlaskleid mit zartem Perlenschmuck erst zehn Jahre zählte, als Andreas Möller sie porträtierte. Damals hatte ihr Vater, Kaiser Karl VI., zwar die Hoffnung auf einen männlichen Erben noch nicht aufgegeben, aber Maria Theresia galt bereits als begehrteste Braut Europas. Daß sie im Jahr 1736 ihren geliebten Franz Stephan von Lothringen heiraten durfte, war gar nicht „gegen jede politische Vernunft". Ihr Vater wollte keinen Prinzen aus einem mächtigen Herrscherhaus, weil er das Aufgehen der habsburgischen Länder in einem anderen Machtbereich befürchtete.

Das Gemälde Möllers befindet sich in der Porträtgalerie zur Geschichte Österreichs auf Schloß Ambras bei Innsbruck.

42 Das Kaiserpaar Franz I. und Maria Theresia mit Familie. Gemälde von Martin van Meytens, 1754/55. (Franz-Karl-Appartement.)

Das Herrscherpaar ist inmitten seiner elf Kinder auf einer Schloßterrasse dargestellt, von der sich der Blick – wie von einer Bühne in die Kulissen – gegen den Ehrenhof von Schönbrunn öffnet. Eine Terrasse mit diesem Ausblick gab es zwar im Schloßbereich nicht, aber offensichtlich war dem Hofmaler Martin van Meytens (1695–1770) – oder der Kaiserin – daran gelegen, die Familie in Schönbrunn darzustellen, wo sich das familiäre Leben ungestört zu entfalten pflegte. Joseph, der etwa dreizehnjährige Kronprinz, gekleidet in ein prächtiges rotgoldenes Hofkleid, steht auf dem Stern des Marmorbodens,

Emperor Francis I's circle. His publication on the botanic garden of Schönbrunn, "Plantarum rariorum horti Caesarii Schoenbrunnensis descriptiones et icones" includes not only "descriptiones", or descriptions, but also "icones", or pictures of rare beauty based on Jacquin's own watercolours (page 64).

Emperor Francis I was keenly interested in the botanic garden and the menagerie. He cultivated ties to both scientists and gardeners, subsidizing research and expeditions as well as scientific publications. In addition, he was a "dilettante" gardener himself, as shown in the ink drawing by Franz Walter. The Emperor served as personal guide when showing his guests through the Dutch Garden and the Menagerie; from the Middle Pavillion, one of the imperial couple's favourite spots, they had a view of the entire grounds. The pavillion had already been conceived by Jadot, but it was not built until 1759 to designs by J. F. Blondel. Vincenz Fischer embellished it with a ceiling mural. The pavillion also contains oil paintings of animals by Franz Fuxeder kept in the menagerie. Incomparably more impressive, however, are the depictions of animals by Johann Georg von Hamilton, dated 1724, that hung in the imperial art gallery. They are both first-class works of art and exact illustrations suitable for a textbook on zoology.

41 Archduchess Maria Theresa at the age of ten. Painting by Andreas Möller, 1727.

If Schmutzer hat not copied this painting in a copperplate engraving dated 1727, one could hardly believe that the pretty archduchess, dressed in a dark blue satin gown decorated with pearls, was only ten years old when Andreas Möller completed her portrait. At the time her father, Emperor Charles VI, hat not yet given up hopes of a male heir, but Maria Theresa was already being regarded as the most highly sought-after bride in all of Europe. When she was finally allowed to marry her beloved Francis of Lorraine in 1736, it was not "in defiance of political reason". Her father was against her marrying the prince of another powerful ruling house because he feared the Hapsburg dominions might be absorbed by a new power centre.

Möller's painting is in the gallery of historical Austrian portraits at Ambras Palace near Innsbruck.

42 The imperial couple Francis I and Maria Theresa with their family. Painting by Martin van Meytens, 1754/55. (Archduke Francis Charles' apartement.)

The sovereign couple is portrayed with its eleven children on a palace terrace, from where the view – like that into stage scenery – opens into the courtyard. In point of fact, no such terrace with this view existed, but obviously the Painter to the Court, Martin van Meytens (1695–1770) – or the Empress herself – was concerned to place the family where home-life was less confined. Crown Prince Joseph, then thirteen years old and dressed in splendid red-and-gold brocade, stands at the center of the star in the marble floor and hence at the center of the picture, although he is turned toward his mother. She, in a lavishly ornamented blue satin gown, is flanked by the two middle sons: in front of her Charles Joseph in the uniform of his Hungarian regiment; behind her Peter Leopold. The father, wearing a Spanish cape of gold brocade, sits between the two eldest daughters: sixteen year-old Maria Anna and twelve year-old Maria

pavillon; elles sont dûes, parait-il, à Franz Fuxeder. Mais les peintures d'animaux de la galerie impériale de peintures exécutées en 1724 par Johann Georg von Hamilton sont sans comparaison bien plus impressionnantes. Ces œuvres artistiques de toute première qualité pourraient servir en même temps d'illustrations à un atlas sur la faune tant elles sonst exactes et vivantes.

41 L'archiduchesse Marie-Thérèse à l'âge de dix ans. Peinture de Andreas Möller, 1727.

S'il n'existait pas une gravure sur cuivre de Schmutzer, datée de 1727, on aurait bien du mal à croire que la jolie archiduchesse, dans sa robe de satin bleu foncé, ne comptait que dix ans lorsqu'Andreas Möller fit son portrait. A ce moment-là, son père, l'empereur Charles VI, n'avait pas encore abandonné tout espoir d'avoir un héritier mâle mais Marie-Thérèse était déjà considérée comme la fiancée la plus convoitée d'Europe. Qu'elle ait eu, en 1736, l'autorisation d'épouser son François de Loraine bien-aimé ne fut pas une décision „contraire à toute raison politique". Son père ne voulait pas qu'elle épouse un prince d'une puissante maison souveraine car il craignait que les états des Habsbourg passent sous un autre sceptre.
Le tableau de Müller se trouve dans la galerie des portraits pour l'histoire de l'Autriche dans le château d'Ambras près d'Innsbruck.

42 Le couple impérial de François Ier et de Marie-Thérèse avec sa famille. Tableau de Martin van Meytens, 1754/55. (Appartement de l'archiduc François-Charles.)

Les souverains sont représentés au milieu de leurs onze enfants sur une terrasse du château ayant vue sur la cour d'Honneur de Schönbrunn. Il n'existait pas de terrasse jouissant de cette vue dans le château mais il est évident que Martin van Meytens (1695–1770), le peintre de la cour, – ou l'impératrice – désirait représenter la famille à Schönbrunn où la vie familiale avait coutume de se dérouler sans contrainte. Joseph, le dauphin d'environ 13 ans, vêtu d'un magnifique habit de cour or rouge se tient debout sur l'étoile du sol de marbre au centre du tableau mais cependant tourné vers sa mère. A côté d'elle qui porte une robe de satin bleu richement orné, nous voyons les deux autres plus grands fils, devant, Charles-Joseph, dans l'uniforme de son régiment hongrois, plus loin derrière, Pierre-Léopold. Les plus âgées des filles sont debout à côté de leur père et portent une robe-manteau de style espagnol en brocart d'or: Marie-Anne, 16 ans et Marie-Christine, 12 ans. Entre ces deux groupes de personnages, nous voyons Ferdinand-Charles né justement en 1754 qui est dans son berceau, entouré de quatre autres filles. A part Joseph et Leopold, aucun de ces enfants n'était particulièrement doué. Les filles n'avaient pas une beauté éclatante, les autres fils n'étaient pas des génies. Cependant, ces enfants de tempérament et de dispositions différents ont donné un caractère particulier à la Cour de Vienne. Si dans le reste de l'Europe toute la vie de la Cour tournait autour de la présente maîtresse du roi, à Vienne, c'était un groupe d'enfants à la santé florissante qui était au centre de la vie de la Cour et grâce à lui, tout naturellement, la rigueur des conventions de l'étiquette a été assouplie et humanisée.

china di Franz Walter. L'imperatore accompagnava personalmente gli ospiti a visitare il giardino olandese e lo zoo; dal padiglione centrale, luogo particolarmente caro alla coppia imperiale, si godeva di una vista impareggiabile. Il padiglione, già progettato da Jadot, fu costruito solo nel 1759 su disegno di J. F. Blondel e il soffitto fu decorato da Vincenzo Fischer. Nel padiglione si trovano numerosi quadri ad olio degli animali che, all'epoca, erano ospitati nel giardino zoologico. Probabilmente i dipinti sono di Francesco Fuxeder. Di incomparabile bellezza sono i dipinti di Giovanni Giorgio von Hamilton del 1724, che provengono dalla Pinacoteca imperiale. Non solo sono dei veri capolavori d'arte, ma potrebbero trovar posto in un libro di zoologia.

41 L'Arciduchessa Maria Teresa all'età di dieci anni. Dipinto di Andreas Möller, 1727.

Se non ci fosse un'incisione su rame di Schmutzer del 1727 che riproducesse questo quadro, non si crederebbe che la bella arciduchessa dall'abito di raso blu, ricamato con perle, avesse dieci anni allorché fu ritratta da Andreas Möller.
A quell'epoca suo padre, l'Imperatore Carlo VI, non aveva ancora rinunciato all'idea di avere un figlio maschio. Già a quel tempo Maria Teresa era considerata una delle donne più desiderabili d'Europa. Nel 1736 sposò l'uomo che amava, Francesco Stefano di Lorena; questo matrimonio non era considerato contrario alla „ragione di stato".
Il padre di Maria Teresa infatti non desiderava avere un genero che provenisse da una casa regnante in quanto ciò avrebbe potuto rappresentare un pericolo per i territori asburgici.
Il quadro di Möller si trova nella „Galleria dei ritratti" di personaggi della storia austriaca del castello Ambras nei pressi di Innsbruck.

42 La coppia imperiale, Francesco I e Maria Teresa con la famiglia. Dipinto di Martin van Meytens, 1754/55. (Appartamento dell'Arciduca Francesco Carlo.)

La coppia imperiale è raffigurata, circondata dagli undici figli, su una terrazza del castello, al di là della quale si apre, come uno scenario, il cortile d'onore di Schönbrunn.
A dire il vero una terrazza con una tale vista non c'era proprio a Schönbrunn, ma il pittore di Corte Martino van Meytens (1695–1770) – o forse l'Imperatrice – ci teneva a rappresentare la famiglia a Schönbrunn, dove si svolgeva, indisturbata, la tranquilla vita familiare. Giuseppe, il Principe ereditario che all'epoca aveva tredici anni, è in piedi, vestito con uno splendido abito rosso dorato. Si noti come egli si ritrovi sul motivo a forma di „stella", del pavimento di marmo che è al centro del quadro. Il volto è tuttavia rivolto verso la madre. Accanto a questa, che è vestita con un abito riccamente decorato di raso azzurro, vi sono i due figli minori. Davanti vediamo Carlo Giuseppe con la divisa del suo reggimento ungherese e molto più indietro Pietro Leopoldo. Accanto al padre, che indossa un mantello spagnolo di broccato dorato, si trovano le figlie maggiori: Maria Anna, di sedici anni, e Maria Cristina, di dodici anni.
Tra questi due gruppi di personaggi, ben distinti, si nota Ferdinando Carlo, nato nel 1754, ancora nella culla, circondato da quattro sorelline. Se si eccettuano Giuseppe e Leopoldo, nessuno dei figli di Maria Teresa era particolarmente dotato. Le ragazze non erano delle grandi bellezze, i maschi non erano dei geni. Tuttavia, grazie ai loro diversi

im Zentrum des Bildes, jedoch der Mutter zugewandt. Neben ihr, die ein reichgeschmücktes blaues Atlaskleid trägt, sehen wir auch die beiden mittleren Söhne, vorne Karl Joseph in der Uniform seines ungarischen Regiments, weiter hinten Peter Leopold. Beim Vater, im spanischen Mantelkleid aus Goldbrokat, stehen die ältesten Töchter: die sechzehnjährige Maria Anna und die zwölfjährige Maria Christine. Zwischen diesen beiden Personengruppen blicken wir auf den erst 1754 geborenen Ferdinand Karl, der im Bettchen liegt, umgeben von vier Schwestern. Außer Joseph und Leopold war keines dieser Kinder außerordentlich begabt. Die Töchter waren nicht strahlend schön, die anderen Söhne keine Genies. Dennoch haben diese Kinder mit ihren ganz verschiedenen Temperamenten und Anlagen dem Wiener Hof einen besonderen Charakter verliehen. Drehten sich die höfischen Gesellschaften des übrigen Europas um die jeweilige Mätresse des Königs, stand in Wien eine blühende Kinderschar im Zentrum des Hofes, durch die wie von selbst die gesellschaftlichen Konventionen gelockert und vermenschlicht wurden.

43 Das Frühstückszimmer in der Südwestecke des Schlosses.

Das Eckkabinett im Westtrakt war (wie auch das Spiegelzimmer, Seiten 46, 47), ein Raum der Privatgemächer Maria Theresias und Franz' I. bis zu deren Übersiedlung in den Osttrakt. Möglicherweise wurde es dann von Kaiserin Maria Josepha, der zweiten Gemahlin Josephs II., als Frühstückszimmer verwendet. Heute schmücken seine Wände Blumenbouquets in vergoldeten Rokokorahmen, die durch goldene Bänder und Maschen miteinander verbunden sind. Die Applikationsstickereien stammen entweder von der Hand Maria Theresias selbst oder sind Arbeiten ihrer Töchter. Die Ausstattung dieses Raumes ist neben der des Porzellanzimmers ein eindrucksvolles Beispiel dafür, daß die Familie der Kaiserin ganz persönlich an der Ausschmückung der Schloßräume Anteil hatte.

44 Die Erzherzoginnen Maria Anna, Maria Christine und Marie Antoinette. (Kinderzimmer.)

Eine Gruppe von Porträts von Töchtern Maria Theresias aus den Jahren 1767/68 schmückt heute das Kinderzimmer im Westflügel, welches zum Appartement der Kaiserin Elisabeth gehörte. Da der Maler dieser Halbfigurbilder unbekannt ist, wurde ihm der Notname „Meister der Erzherzoginnenporträts" gegeben.
Maria Anna, die Älteste, kam zur Welt, als ihre Mutter noch Erzherzogin war und wurde von ihr als Sorgenkind besonders geliebt: Sie war leicht verwachsen und häufig krank. So widmete sie sich nicht nur dem Theaterspielen und Zeichnen, sondern auch der Lektüre und dem Sammeln und Katalogisieren von Münzen wie ihr Vater und ihr Großvater Kaiser Karl VI. Im Jahre 1766 entschloß sie sich, als Äbtissin in das Adelige Damenstift in Prag einzutreten, hielt sich aber zu Lebzeiten der Mutter meist in Wien auf.
Von Maria Christines künstlerischer Begabung war schon die Rede. Als einzige der Töchter durfte sie aus Liebe heiraten, allerdings auch erst den zweiten Kandidaten und erst 1766, als ihr Vater bereits gestorben war. Mit ihrem Mann, dem sächsischen Prinzen Albert, lebte sie einige Jahre in Preßburg, ab 1780 in Brüssel. Gemeinsam bauten sie jene wundervolle graphische Sammlung auf, die heute, nach ihm Albertina benannt, Weltruhm genießt.

Christine. Between the two groups we find Ferdinand Charles, who was not born until 1754, lying in his crib and surrounded by four sisters. Except for Joseph and Leopold, none of the children were particularly gifted. The daughters were not radiant beauties; nor were the other sons touched by genius. Nonetheless these children with their variety of temperaments and talents gave the Vienna court its particular character. Whereas the courtly societies of the rest of Europe tended to centre around the King's mistress, in Vienna a group of children in the full bloom of their youth was the centre of attention which automatically relaxed and humanised the rigid social conventions of courtly life.

43 The Breakfast Room in the southwest corner of the palace.

This room on the west wing (like the Mirror Room, pages 46, 47) belonged to the private apartments of Maria Theresa and Francis I until they moved into the east wing. It was possibly used by Empress Maria Josepha, the second wife of Joseph II, as a breakfastroom. Today the walls are adorned with bouquets of flowers in gilt rococo frames connected to one another by gold ribbon. The appliqué embroidery is said to be the work of either Maria Theresa herself or her daugthers. The furnishings of this room – next to those of the Porcelain Room – bear eloquent witness to the personal contributions made by the imperial family toward the interior decoration of the palace.

44 The Archduchesses Maria Anna, Maria Christine, and Marie Antoinette. (Children's room.)

The children's room which was part of Empress Elisabeth's apartments in the west wing is adorned with a collection of portraits of Maria Theresa's daughters from 1767/68. Because the name of the artist who painted these half-length portraits is unknown, he is referred to as the "Master of the Archduchesses' Portraits". Maria Anna, the eldest, was born while her mother was still an archduchess and was especially loved by her as a problem child: she was slightly misshapen and frequently ill. In addition to being well-versed in theatre and drawing, she was also well-read and emulated her father and her grandfather, Emperor Charles VI, collecting and cataloguing coins. In 1766 she decided to become abbess of a convent in Prague for ladies of rank, but remained mostly in Vienna until her mother's death. Reference has already been made to Maria Christine's artistic talent. She was the only daughter who was permitted to marry for love – although only her second suitor and not until 1766, after her father had already died. She lived with her husband, Prince Albert of Saxony, for a few years in Pressburg before moving to Brussels in 1780. Together they built up the world-renowned collection of art called, after her husband, the "Albertina".
At the age of fifteen, Maria Antonia left her almost middle-class Viennese home for the luxurious and extravagant court at Versailles. Her mother's many admonishing letters testify to the latter's concern. For a few all-too frivolous years her beauty, as the portrait would lead one to expect, charmed everyone. Only belatedly did she discover responsibility and strength of character by proving herself, throughout the ordeal of imprisonment and up to her execution by the guillotine, a true daughter of her great mother.

43 La salle du petit déjeuner dans l'angle sud-ouest du château.

Le cabinet du coin de l'aile ouest fut (comme également la salle des Glaces, pages 46, 47) une pièce des appartements privés de Marie-Thérèse et de François Ier jusqu'à ce qu'ils s'installent dans l'aile est. Il est possible que l'impératrice Marie-Josèphe, la deuxième épouse de Joseph II, s'en soit servi pour y prendre son petit déjeuner. Aujourd'hui, ses murs sont ornés de bouquets de fleurs dans des cadres rococo dorés reliés les uns aux autres par des rubans et des nœuds dorés. Les broderies d'application ont été exécutées par Marie-Thérèse elle-même ou par ses filles. L'aménagement de cette pièce est une preuve impressionnante de la part que la famille de l'impératrice prenait personellement à la décoration des pièces du château.

44 Les archiduchesses Marie-Anne, Marie-Christine et Marie-Antoinette. (Chambre des enfants.)

Une série de portraits de filles de Marie-Thérèse exécutés entre 1765 et 1767 orne aujourd'hui la chambre d'enfants qui faisait partie de l'appartement de l'impératrice Elisabeth. Comme le peintre de ces portraits en buste est inconnu, on lui a donné le nom de circonstance „Maître des portraits des archiduchesses". Marie-Thérèse avait une affection particulière pour l'aînée qui lui causa beaucoup de soucis; en effet, Marie-Anne était légèrement difforme et de santé fragile. Aussi, elle ne se consacra pas seulement à jouer du théâtre et à dessiner, mais aussi à la lecture et à faire collection de pièces de monnaies qu'elle cataloguait comme son père et son grand-père l'empereur Charles VI. En 1766, elle se décida à entrer comme abbesse au chapitre des Dames nobles de Prague. Nous avons déjà parlé des dons artistique de Marie-Christine. Ce fut la seule des filles à pouvoir se marier par amour, quoique seulement avec le deuxième candidat et uniquement en 1766 lorsque son père fut mort. Elle vécut quelques années à Presbourg avec son mari le prince saxon Albert, puis à partir de 1780, à Bruxelles. Ils créerent ensemble cette magnifique collection qui aujourd'hui est nommé d'après lui, l'Albertina et jouit d'une réputation mondiale.
Marie-Antoinette passa à 15 ans de la chambre d'enfants presque bourgeoise de Vienne à la cour luxueuse et dépensière de Versailles. Cela causa bien des soucis à sa mère comme il ressort de bien des lettres d'admonition qu'elle lui écrivit. Sa beauté que le portrait de Schönbrunn nous laisse pressentir triompha pendant quelques années par trop insouciantes. Elle n'acquit que trop tard le sens des responsabilités et la grandeur de caractère, mais les conserva en prison et dans la mort sur l'échafaud où elle se montra digne de la grandeur de sa mère.

temperamenti e interessi, si manifestò un'impronta particolare alla Corte imperiale viennese. Mentre presso le altre società aristocratiche in Europa tutto ruotava intorno alle favorite del Re, alla Corte di Vienna una schiera di bambini era al centro degli interessi, che riusciorono a rendere meno rigide e più umane le convenzioni sociali.

43 Stanza della prima colazione nell'angolo a sudovest del castello.

La piccola stanza d'angolo nell'ala occidentale (così come la stanza degli specchi, pagg. 46, 47) faceva parte degli appartamenti privati della coppia imperiale fino a quando questa non si trasferì nell'ala orientale. Pare che questa stanza fosse adibita alla prima colazione dell'Imperatrice Maria Giuseppina, seconda moglie di Giuseppe II. Oggi adornano le pareti della stanza dei motivi di fiori in cornici dorate di stile Rococò. Ogni cornice è legata all'altra da nastri e fiocchi dorati. I ricami sono stati eseguiti dalla stessa Maria Teresa e dalle figlie.
L'arredamento di questa stanza, così come quello della stanza delle porcellane, mostra come la famiglia dell'Imperatrice si occupasse personalmente della decorazione dei suoi appartamenti.

44 Le Arciduchesse Maria Anna, Maria Cristina e Maria Antonietta. (Stanza dei bambini.)

Una serie di ritratti delle figlie di Maria Terese (degli anni 1765–1767) adorna le pareti della camera dei bambini nell'ala ovest. Questa stanza feceva parte degli appartamenti dell'Imperatrice Elisabetta. L'autore dei ritratti, a mezzo busto è ignoto; per questa ragione egli fu semplicemente chiamato „maestro dei ritratti delle Arciduchesse". Maria Anna, la maggiore, nacque quando la madre era ancora Arciduchessa; fu aparticolamente amata in quanto era malaticcia e aveva dei disturbi della crescita. Si interessò molto al teatro e al disegno leggeva con grande passione, raccoglieva e ordinava monete, interesse ereditato dal padre e dal nonno, l'Imperatore Carlo VI. Nel 1766 divenne Badessa del convento delle nobili dame di Praga. Finchè la madre fu viva abitò però lo più a Vienna. Si è già accennato al fatto che Maria Cristina avesse molta attitudine per l'arte. Fu l'unica a sposare l'uomo che amava, il secondo partito propostole. Il matrimonio avvenne nel 1766, cioè dopo la morte del padre. Visse col marito, il principe Alberto di Sassonia, per alcuni anni a Bratislava e poi, dal 1780, a Bruxelles. Insieme realizzarono quella meravigliosa collezione che va sotto il nome di „Albertina".
Maria Antonia si trasferí, all'età di quindici anni, dall'atmosfera quasi borghese della corte viennese a quella lussosa e sontuosa di Versailles. La madre era seriamente preoccupata di questo fatto, come testimoniano molte lettere scritte alla figliola. Per qualche anno spensierato la sua bellezza trionfò, come possiamo vedere dal ritratto di Schönbrunn. Troppo tardi Maria Antonietta divenne responsabile e rifessiva; tuttavia in prigione e in occasione della morte sul patibolo, si comportò come si addice alla figlia di una tale grande madre.

Marie Antoinette wurde fünfzehnjährig aus der fast bürgerlichen Wiener Kinderstube an den luxuriösen und verschwenderischen Hof von Versailles versetzt. Das bereitete ihrer Mutter nicht geringe Sorgen, wie aus vielen ermahnenden Briefen hervorgeht. Ein paar allzu unbeschwerte Jahre lang triumphierte ihre Schönheit, die das Schönbrunner Porträt schon erwarten läßt. Zu spät fand sie zu Verantwortung und Charaktergröße, bewährte sich aber in Gefangenschaft und Tod am Schafott als Tochter ihrer großen Mutter.

44   Nikolausbescherung in der kaiserlichen Familie, um 1760.

Noch weit bis ins 19. Jahrhundert war es auch in Wien nur zu Nikolo üblich, die Kinder zu beschenken. Zu Weihnachten gab es im 18. Jahrhundert in einem Wiener Bürgerhaus weder einen Christbaum noch Geschenke. So war es auch in der kaiserlichen Familie. Das so ganz und gar unhöfische Bildchen vom Nikoloabend gibt dafür ein beredtes Zeugnis. Auch bei der Erziehung ihrer Kinder ließ Maria Theresia nicht jene Oberflächlichkeit und Willkür gelten, die an Fürstenhöfen oft an den Tag gelegt wurde, sondern sorgte für Strenge und gutbürgerliche Regelmäßigkeit. Als eine Kammerfrau einmal einwandte, daß die kaiserlichen Prinzen früher nie geschlagen worden seien, sagte Maria Theresia: „Sie waren auch danach!". Zur sorgfältigen Erziehung gehörte – wie bei „höheren Töchtern" – die musikalische und zeichnerische Ausbildung.
Das kleine Bildchen hat Maria Christine, von ihrer Mutter zärtlich Mimi genannt, gemalt, wobei sie als Vorlage für die Komposition einen holländischen Stich gewählt hatte. Ganz links hat sie sich selbst porträtiert, wie sie eben dem kleinen Bruder Ferdinand mit der Rute droht. Marie Antoinette zeigt beglückt ihre neue Puppe, während der Jüngste, Maximilian Franz, sich am Lebkuchen delektiert. Der behäbig-ernste Vater und die resolute Mutter stellen in der Tat nicht dar, was man sich unter Römisch-kaiserlichen Majestäten vorstellt, die vor der Öffentlichkeit von einem Zeremoniell beherrscht waren, das ihnen keinen freien Schritt, kein ungezwungenes Wort gestatten wollte.

46/47   Das Spiegelzimmer.

Im Grundriß Fischers von Erlach (Seite 39) sehen wir zwei große Räume an der Gartenseite des Westflügels, von denen der eine später unterteilt wurde, der andere damals „Chambre à coucher" Kaiser Josephs I. hieß und seit Maria Theresias Zeiten „Spiegelzimmer" genannt wird. Die einheitliche weißgolden gefaßte Holzausstattung, die weißen Marmorkamine und die zwölf vergoldeten Bronzegirandolen entsprechen in ihren spielerischen Formen Pacassis Konzept einer Umgestaltung des Barockschlosses im Geschmack des Rokoko. Den weiß-goldenen Grundakkord beleben rotgepolsterte Hocker und Sessel sowie blauweißes, ostasiatisches Porzellan.
Das Kaiserpaar übersiedelte im Jahre 1747 in den Ostflügel des Schlosses und überließ die westlichen Räume der Prinzessin Charlotte von Lothringen, Schwester des Kaisers, die von 1745 bis 1754 in Wien lebte. Später gab hier Kaiserin Maria Josepha, die zweite Gemahlin Josephs II., Audienzen. Im 19. Jahrhundert fand das Spiegelzimmer als Speisesaal Verwendung.

44   The imperial family celebrating the feast of St. Nicholas, c. 1760.

Until far into the nineteenth century it was the custom also in Vienna to give presents to children only on St. Nicholas (6th December), where as at Christmas there was neither a Christmas tree nor presents. That was true of the imperial family as well, to which the painting, so atypical of court life, bears eloquent witness. In matters of the children's upbringing, Maria Theresa emphasized strictness and the bourgeois virtue of consistency in contrast to the superficiality and capriciousness that were the rule at other princely courts. When a chambermaid once commented that the crown princes had never been struck in former times, Maria Theresa retorted that "they also turned out accordingly!" The study of music and drawing were also important constituents of the children's conscientious rearing, as befitted "privileged daughters". Using a Dutch engraving as a model this small picture was created by Maria Christine, affectionately called "Mimi" by her mother. At the far left she has depicted herself threatening her younger brother Ferdinand with a switch. Maria Antoinette is showing off her new doll, while the youngest child, Maximilian Francis, enjoys the delicious gingerbread. The portly, sober father and resolute mother bear little resemblance to the imperial majesties whose public lives were bound completely by ceremonial dictates.

46/47   The Room of Mirrors.

Fischer von Erlach's ground plan (page 39) includes two large rooms on the garden side of the west wing, one of which was later subdivided, while the other – once Joseph I's "chambre à coucher" – has been known as the "Room of Mirrors" since Maria Theresa's time. The playful forms of the uniform white paneling with gold-leaf ornamentation, the white marble fireplaces and the twelve gilded bronze candelabra conform to Pacassi's ideas for the redecoration of the baroque palace in the style of rococo. The basic white-and-gold pattern is varied and enlivened by the red upholstery of the chairs and stools and the blue-and-white East Asian porcelain.
The imperial couple moved into the east wing of the palace in 1747, leaving the west rooms they had vacated to Princess Charlotte of Lorraine, the Emperor's sister, who resided in Vienna from 1745 to 1754. It was later the audience-room of Empress Maria Josepha, the second wife of Joseph II. In the nineteenth century the Mirror Room was also used as a dining hall.

Stuck und Skulpturen im Inneren der Gloriette.
Stucco work and sculptures inside the Gloriette.
Stucs et sculptures de l'intérieur de la Gloriette.
Lavori in stucco e sculture all'interno della Gloriette.

Napoleons Einzug in Schönbrunn 1809. Stich von François Aubertin (Ausschnitt).
Napoleon's entrée in Schönbrunn in 1809. Engraving by François Aubertin (detail).
Entrée de Napoléon à Schönbrunn en 1809. Gravure de François Aubertin (détail).
Ingresso ufficiale a Schönbrunn di Napoleone. Incisione di François Aubertin (particolare).

Kaiser Napoleon I. und Kaiserin Marie Luise, geborene Erzherzogin von Österreich. Miniaturen auf Elfenbein von Jean-Baptiste Isabey, 1810.
Emperor Napoleon I and Empress Marie Luise, née Archduchess of Austria. Miniatures on ivory by Jean-Baptiste Isabey, 1810.
L'empereur Napoléon Ier et l'impératrice Marie-Louise, née archiduchesse d'Autriche. Miniatures sur ivoire de Jean-Baptiste Isabey, 1810.
L'Imperatore Napoleone I e l'Imperatrice Maria Luisa, nata Arciduchessa d'Austria. Miniature su avorio di Jean-Baptiste Isabey, 1810.

Das Napoleon-Zimmer.
Napoleon Room.
La chambre de Napoléon.
La stanza di Napoleone.

Kaiser Franz Joseph I. und Kronprinz Rudolf, umgeben von Mitgliedern der Dynastie, in der kleinen Galerie, 1863.
Emperor Francis Joseph I. and his son, Crown Prince Rudolph, surrounded by other members of the Hapsburg dynasty, in the Small Gallery, 1863.
L'empereur François – Joseph Ier et le prince héretier Rodolphe entourés par des membres de la dynastie, dans la petite galerie, 1863.
L'imperatore Francesco Giuseppe I. e l'Infante Rodolfo intorno ad alcuni membri della dinastia imperiale nella Piccola Galleria.

Kaiser Franz Joseph I. an seinem Schreibtisch. Gemälde von Franz Matsch, um 1915.
Emperor Francis Joseph I at his desk. Painting by Franz Matsch, c. 1915.
L'empereur François-Joseph Ier à son bureau, tableau de Franz Matsch, vers 1915.
L'Imperatore Francesco Giuseppe I seduto alla scrivania. Dipinto di Franz Matsch. Intorno al 1915.

Wohn- und Schlafräume des Kaisers Franz Joseph und seiner Gemahlin Elisabeth.
Living quarters of Emperor Francis Joseph and his wife, Empress Elizabeth.
Appartements et chambre à coucher de l'empereur François-Joseph et de son épouse Elisabeth.
Stanze di soggiorno e camere da letto dell'Imperatore Francesco Giuseppe I e della sua consorte Elisabetta.

Stukkaturen in den beiden Galerien.
Stucco-works in both Galleries.
Stucs dans les deux galeries.
Stucchi in entrambe le Gallerie.

44 La fête de la Saint-Nicolas dans la famille impériale, vers 1760.

Jusque vers la moitié du 19ème siècle, il fut habituel à Vienne de ne faire des cadeaux aux enfants que pour la Saint-Nicolas. Au 18ème siècle, à Noël, dans une maison bourgeoise viennoise, il n'y avait ni arbre de Noël ni cadeaux. C'était également le cas dans la famille impériale. Le tableau tout à fait naturel de la fête de la Saint-Nicolas en porte un témoignage éloquent. Pour l'éducation de ses enfants, Marie-Thérèse veilla à ce que la sévérité et un ordre bourgeois règnent. Comme une femme de chambre protestait une fois que les princes impériaux n'avaient jamais été battus auparavant, Marie-Thérèse réplique: „on a vu ce que cela a donné!".

Le petit tableau a été peint par Marie-Christine que sa mère appelait tendrement Mimi; elle avait choisi comme modèle de la composition une gravure hollandaise. Elle s'est représentée tout à gauche menaçant son petit frère Ferdinand des verges. Marie-Antoinette montre enchantée sa nouvelle poupée tandis que le plus jeune, Maximilien-François, fait ses délices de pain d'épice. Le père sérieux et paisible et la mère résolue ne ressemblent en effet pas aux majestés impériales Romaines qui, en public, étaient soumises à une étiquette qui ne leur permettait ni de faire un pas librement ni de prononcer un mot sans contrainte.

46/47 La salle des Glaces.

Sur le plan de Fischer von Erlach (page 39), nous voyons deux grandes pièces de l'aile ouest donnant sur le jardin; l'une fut divisée plus tard en deux l'autre fut appelée alors „chambre à coucher" de l'empereur Joseph Ier et a été nommée depuis l'époque de Marie-Thérèse „la salle des Glaces". La décoration uniformément blanc et or, les cheminees de marbre blanc et les douze girandoles de bronze doré sont conformes par leurs formes enjouées à la conception de Pacassi lorsqu'il effectua des transformations dans le château baroque pour le mettre au goût du rococo. L'accord de base blanc or est égayé par des tabourets et des sièges rembourrés de couleur rouge de même que par de la porcelaine bleue et blanche de l'Asie orientale.

Le couple impérial déménagea en 1747 dans l'aile est du château. Plus tard, l'impératrice Marie-Josèphe, épouse de Joseph II, y donna des audiences. Au 19ème siècle, la salle des Glaces fut utilisée comme salle à manger.

48/49 La Grande Galerie; l'impératrice Marie-Thérèse et l'ordre du mérite qu'elle a créé.

Les deux galeries, cœur de la partie du château que Marie-Thérèse fit transformer par Pacassi, pouvaient être employées des façons les plus différentes. La Grande Galerie de plus de 40 m de long et d'à peine 10 m de large servait de salle des fêtes pour les grandes réceptions et les bals, mais habituellement, de première salle d'attente (antichambre) d'où l'on était conduit dans les salles d'audience. La Petite Galerie (page 45) était la scène de fêtes enfantines, de représentations musicales, de mascarades et de jeux familiaux. Les deux galeries prisent leur aspect solennel actuel lors de l'achèvement des fresques et des stucs de G. Guglielmi et d'Albert Bolla en 1761. Les couleurs des pièces sont remarquables (page 45). Les fresques multicolores du plafond planent au-dessus d'une clarté éblouissante de blanc et d'or qui est

44 La festa di San Nicolò presso la famiglia imperiale, intorno al 1760.

Ancora nel XIX secolo c'era l'abitudine, a Vienna, di fare dei regali ai bambini solo il giorno di S. Nicolò. Nel XVIII secolo, in occasione del Natale, nelle famiglie borghesi, non si preparava l'albero e non ci si scambiavano i regali. La stessa abitudine vigeva per la famiglia imperiale. Il quadretto, per nulla regale, che raffigura la sera di S. Nicolò, è una preziosa testimonianza di questa consuetudine. Nell'educazione dei propri figli, Maria Teresa non lasciò mai posto alla superficialità e alla protervia, cosa che accadeva spesso alle corti principesche, ma si preoccupò affinchè i figli crescessero all'insegna della severità e dei sani principi borghesi. Una volta, una cameriera fece notare all'Imperatrice che i principi reali, un tempo, non venivano mai picchiati. Maria Teresa rispose: „E si sono visti i bei risultati."

Faceva parte di un'educazione accurata, specialmente per quanto riguarda le ragazze, una seria cultura musicale ed artistica. Questo quadretto fu dipinto da Maria Cristina, Mimì, come la chiamava sua madre. Modello per questa composizione fu un'incisione olandese. A sinistra la ragazzina ha rappresentato se stessa nell'atto di minacciare con la verga il fratellino minore Ferdinando. Maria Antonietta mostra felice la sua nuova bambola, mentre il più piccolo dei fratelli, Massimiliano Francesco, mangia del panforte. Il padre, corpulento, dall'aria severa, e la madre, donna molta decisa, non assomigliano per nulla alle maestà del Sacro-Romano Impero, sottoposte, in pubblico, ad un rigido cerimonale, che non permetteva loro di fare un passo liberamente e che non consentiva loro una parola in più di quelle previste.

46/47 La Stanza degli specchi.

Nel progetto di Fischer von Erlach (pag. 39) vediamo due grandi locali nella parte verso il giardino dell'ala occidentale. Uno di questi locali fu diviso più tardi, l'altro prese il nome di „chambre à coucher". A partire dall'epoca di Maria Teresa venne chiamato „stanza degli specchi".

Le pareti bianche e oro, ornate con decorazioni sovrapposte in legno, i camini di marmo bianco e i dodici candelieri in bronzo dorato rendono bene, grazie al loro manierismo, l'idea di Pacassi che intendeva trasformare il castello, originariamente barocco, in uno di stile rococò.

Degli sgabelli e delle poltrone, rivestiti di tessuto rosso, e delle porcellane bianco-azzurre, provenienti dalla Cina orientale, movimentano il colore di base, bianco dorato. La coppia imperiale si trasferì nel 1747 nell'ala orientale del castello e lasciò le stanze occidentali alla principessa Carlotta di Lorena, sorella dell'Imperatore, che visse a Vienna dal 1745 al 1754. Più tardi l'Imperatrice Maria Giuseppina, seconda moglie di Giuseppe II, utilizzò questa stanza per le udienze. Nel XIX secolo essa fu trasformata in stanza da pranzo.

48/49   Die Große Galerie; Kaiserin Maria Theresia und der von ihr gestiftete militärische Verdienstorden.

Die beiden Galerien, Herzstück des Umbaus, den Maria Theresia durch Pacassi durchführen ließ, konnten in verschiedenster Weise verwendet werden. Die Große Galerie, über 40 m lang und knapp 10 m breit, diente als Festsaal bei großen Empfängen und Bällen, gewöhnlich aber als erster Wartesaal (Antikammer), von dem man über die beiderseits gelegenen zweiten Antikammern in die Audienzräume geführt wurde. Die Kleine Galerie (Seite 45) war der Schauplatz von Kinderfesten, Musikdarstellungen, Maskeraden und Spielen der großen Familie. Das heutige festliche Aussehen erhielten die beiden Galerien erst mit Fertigstellung der Fresken und Stukkaturen von G. Guglielmi bzw. Albert Bolla im Jahr 1761. Während die Gliederung des Raumes der Großen Galerie von mächtigen korinthischen Pilastern übernommen wird, fällt diese Aufgabe in der Kleinen Galerie vorspringenden Wandteilen zu, die nicht von Kapitälen abgeschlossen werden, sondern sich in fließenden Übergängen mit dem Gesims und den Bögen der Decke verbinden (Seite 45). Bemerkenswert ist die Farbigkeit der Räume: Die bunte Deckenmalerei schwebt über einer flimmernden weißgoldenen Helligkeit, die durch die großen Kristallspiegel gesteigert und erweitert wird. Die vergoldeten Bronzegirandolen gehören zur originalen Ausstattung, die Luster traten erst während der Regierungszeit Kaiser Franz Josephs anstelle älterer und wurden um 1900 elektrifiziert.

Das mittlere Fresko veranschaulicht allegorisch die österreichischen Kronländer, die dem ganz natürlich dargestellten Herrscherpaar huldigen; die beiden seitlichen stellen die Werke des Krieges (mit Szenen aus dem Siebenjährigen Krieg; Seite 10) denen des Friedens (Kunst und Wissenschaft) gegenüber.

Schloß Schönbrunn wird meistens in einem Atemzug mit dem Namen Maria Theresia genannt. Tatsächlich hat sie Schönbrunn zum politischen und gesellschaftlichen Mittelpunkt der österreichischen Erbländer gemacht und ihm jene Bedeutung verliehen, die uns heute noch gegenwärtig ist. Die „Erste Dame Europas" tritt uns hier in einem kostbaren Kleid aus Brabanter Klöppelspitzen entgegen. Auf dem Tisch vor ihr liegen die heiligen Kronen Ungarns und Böhmens, mit denen sie gekrönt wurde, und als Zeichen ihrer höchsten Würde die Reichskrone, Insigne ihres Gatten Franz I. Als er 1745 zum Kaiser gewählt und gekrönt wurde, sagten die Leute: „Der Mann der Königin von Ungarn wird deutscher Kaiser." Sie ist also die „Augustissima", wie sie Graf Friedrich August Harrach, der böhmische Oberste Kanzler, nannte. Das Bildnis stammt von ihrem Hofmaler Martin van Meytens.

Viele Jahre ihrer Regierungszeit führte Maria Theresia Krieg. Den Überfall des Preußenkönigs Friedrich II. konnten die österreichischen Truppen mit letzter Kraft zurückschlagen; Schlesien ging verloren. Ein Jahrzehnt lang wurde das Heer reformiert und gerüstet, um Schlesien zurückzugewinnen: Im Siebenjährigen Krieg (1756–1763) setzte Maria Theresia mit neuen Verbündeten nochmals alles auf eine Karte und verlor zuletzt einen schon fast gewonnenen Krieg. Zu den großen Einzelsiegen der Österreicher zählen jene von Kolin am 18. Juni 1757 und Kunersdorf. Den Tag von Kolin bezeichnete die Kaiserin in einem Brief an den siegreichen Feldmarschall Leopold Graf Daun (1705–1766) als „Geburtstag der Monarchie" und stiftete den Militär-Maria-Theresien-Orden. Als erste erhielten ihn Daun und ihr Schwager Karl von Lothringen. Dennoch stand dieser Verdienstorden allen „Oberofficiers von dem höchsten bis zum niedrigsten, mithin inclusive der Fähndriche, ohne auf ihre Reli-

48/49   The Great Gallery; Empress Maria Theresa and the military decoration founded by her.

The two galleries, the heart of the renovations Maria Theresa had carried out by Pacassi, had numerous uses. The Great Gallery, over forty meters long and ten meters wide, served as a festival hall for large receptions and balls. Otherwise it was employed as a waiting-room, or "anticamera", which opened into either of the two adjoining antechambers leading to the audience-rooms. The Small Gallery (page 45) was used by the large imperial family for children's parties, music, masquerades, and games. The present festive appearance of the galleries is due to the frescoes by G. Guglielmi and the stucco-work by Albert Bolla completed in 1761. Wheras the Great Gallery is subdivided by powerful Corinthian pilasters, in the Small Gallery this function is assumed by projecting wall panels which, rather than being surmounted by capitals, gradually merge into the cornice and ceiling arches in a fluent transition (page 45). The colourfulness of the rooms deserves remark: the colourful frescoes seem to hover above a scintillating pattern of white and gold intensified and extended by crystal mirrors. The gilded bronze candelabra are part of the original furnishings; the chandeliers replaced older ones during the reign of Emperor Francis Joseph and were electrified about 1900.

The middle fresco is an allegorical depiction of the Austrian crown-lands paying homage to the naturalistically portrayed sovereign couple. The two frescoes flanking it juxtapose military accomplishments (with scenes from the Seven Years' War; page 10) with those of peace (art and science).

The Palace of Schönbrunn is mentioned almost always in connection with Maria Theresa. Indeed, it was she who made Schönbrunn the political and social hub of the Austrian dominions, thereby endowing it with a significance we can still sense today. The "First Lady of Europe" is depicted here in a costly gown of bobbin-lace from Brabant. On the table before her are the holy crowns of Hungary and Bohemia, with which she was crowned, as well as the symbol of her highest rank and the insignia of her husband, the Imperial Crown. When Francis I was elected and crowned Emperor in 1745, it was said of him: "The husband of the Queen of Hungary has become the German Emperor." For that reason she was called the "Augustissima" by the First Chancellor of Bohemia, Count Friedrich August Harrach. The painting is by Martin van Meytens.

For many years of her reign Maria Theresa was involved in waging war. The troops of Austria were only barely able to repel King Frederick II of Prussia's invasion. Silesia had to be ceded. For a whole decade the army was reformed and re-equipped in order to win back the lost territory: in the Seven Years' War (1756–1763), Maria Theresa, this time with new allies, finally lost a war she might nearly have won. Among the great individual battles decided in favour of the Austrians were those at Kolin on 18th June 1757, and at Kunersdorf. In a letter to the victorious Field Marshal Count Leopold Daun (1705–1766), Maria Theresa christened the battle of Kolin the "birthday of the monarchy" and subsequently founded the Military Order named after her. Its first recipients were Daun and her brother-in-law, Charles of Lorraine. Nevertheless the distinction was open to all "commissioned officers irrespective of rank and including ensigns, and without regard to religion, rank, origins, or years of service". Almost one third of the officers who were to become Knights of Maria Theresa were actually of middle-class origins.

augmentée et amplifée par les grandes glaces en cristal. Les girandoles de bronze doré font partie de la décoration originale; les lustres ont été installés seulement pendant le règne de François-Joseph à la place de plus anciens et ont été électrifiés vers 1900. La fresque centrale représente une allégorie des états héréditaires autrichiens qui rendent tout naturellement hommage aux souverains représentés; les deux fresques latérales confrontent la guerre (avec des scènes de la guerre de Sept ans; page 10) aux bienfaits de la paix: art et sciences.

La plupart du temps, on homme d'un trait le château de Schönbrunn et Marie-Thérèse. C'est qu'effectivement elle a fait de Schönbrunn le centre politique et mondain des états héréditaires autrichiens et lui a conféré cette importance qui nous est encore sensible aujourd'hui. La „première dame de l'Europe" nous apparait ici dans une robe précieuse de dentelle aux fuseaux du Brabant. Sur la table devant elle sont posées les saintes couronnes de Hongrie et de Bohême dont elle fut couronnée et, en tant que marque de sa plus haute dignité, la couronne impériale, insigne de son époux François Ier. Lorsqu'il fut élu et couronné empereur en 1745, on dit: „Le mari de la reine de Hongrie devient empereur allemand". Marie-Thérèse est aussi l' „Augustissima" comme la nommait le chancelier de Bohême, le comte Friedrich August Harrach. Le portrait a été peint par Martin van Meytens, son peintre de la cour.

Marie-Thérèse fit la guerre pendant bien des annéees de son règne. Par un dernier effort, les troupes autrichiennes repoussèrent l'attaque par surprise du roi de Prusse, Fréderic II; la Silésie fut perdue. Pendant une dizaine d'années, l'armée fut réformée et pour regagner la Silésie: pendant la guerre de Sept ans (1756–1763), Marie-Thérèse mise de nouveau tout sur une carte avec de nouveaux alliés et perdit finalement une guerre déjà presque gagnée. Parmi les grandes victoires remportées par les Autrichiens, nous citerons celles de Kolin le 18 juin 1757 et de Kunersdorf. La journée de Kolin fut désignée par l'impératrice dans une lettre au feld-marechal comte Leopold Daun victorieux (1705–1766) comme le „jour de la naissance de la monarchie" et elle fonda l'ordre militaire de Marie-Thérèse. Son beau-frère Charles de Lorraine et Daun furent les premiers décorés. Cependant cet ordre du mérite pouvait être décerné aux „officiers supérieurs du rang le plus élevé au moins élevé, y compris les aspirants, sans faire aucune distinction de religion, de rang, de naissance ni d'années de service". Presque un tiers des officiers qui devaient plus tard devenir chevaliers de l'ordre de Marie-Thérèse étaient vraiment d'origine bourgeoise.

48/49 La Grande Galleria; l'Imperatrice Maria Teresa e l'ordine al merito da lei istituito.

Entrambe le gallerie, cuore di Schönbrunn, volute da Maria Teresa quando affidò a Pacassi la rielaborazione del progetto del castello, venivano variamente utilizzate. La Grande Galleria (più di 40 m di lunghezza e 10 m circa di larghezza) serviva come salone di rappresentanza durante i ricevimenti e le feste. Di solito però era la prima anticamera (ne seguivano altre due) che conduceva nelle sale delle udienze.

La Piccola Galleria (pag. 45) veniva adibita a feste per i bambini, a rappresentazioni musicali, a mascherate, ai giochi della famiglia. Entrambe le gallerie debbono il loro aspetto cosí imponente agli affreschi e agli stucchi rispettivamente di G. Guglielmi e Alberto Bolla. Queste decorazioni furono ultimate nel 1761. La Grande Galleria è suddivisa da potenti colonne corinzie; per la Piccola Galleria invece sono state utilizzate delle mezze pareti che non si conchiudono con capitelli, ma che sono armonicamente collegate al soffitto grazie ad archi ed a cornicioni (pag. 45). Si noti la ricchezza dei colori di questi ambienti: gli affreschi del soffitto, cosí variopinti, sovrastano il bianco e oro splendente, che ottiene particolare spicco e risalto grazie a grandi specchi di cristallo. I candelieri in bronzo dorato fanno parte dell'arredamento originale, mentre i lampadari, che funzionano a luce elettrica, hanno sostituito, intorno al 1900, i precedenti, più antichi.

L'affresco centrale rappresenta allegoricamente i territori della corona austriaca, che rendono omaggio alla coppia imperiale mentre i due affreschi laterali raffigurano i fatti di guerra dei Sette anni (pag. 10) e i fatti di pace (arte e scienza).

Il castello di Schönbrunn e il nome di Maria Teresa sono, per così dire, sinonimi. Infatti il castello di Schönbrunn divenne, in quel periodo, il centro politico e mondano dei territori austriaci, e in questo modo acquistò quella grandissima importanza di cui si fregia ancor oggi. La „prima dama d'Europa" è raffigurata in uno splendido abito di tombolo, tipico del Brabante. Sul tavolino sono poggiate le corone di Ungheria e di Boemia, con le quali fu incoronata, e, come segno della sua massima dignità, la corona del regno, insegna del marito Francesco I. Nel 1745, quando questi fu incoronato imperatore, la gente disse: „Il marito della Regina di Ungheria diventa Imperatore germanico". Maria Teresa è dunque la „augustissima"; così la definì il Conte Frederico Augusto Harrach, massimo Cancelliere di Boemia. Il ritratto fu dipinto dal suo pittore di Corte Martin van Meytens.

Molti anni del regno di Maria Teresa sono stati caratterizzati da guerre. Le truppe austriache riuscirono a fatica a respingere l'attatco del Re di Prussia, Federico II; andò persa la Slesia. Per un decennio si armò e si rinnovò l'esercito per riconquistare questo territorio. Nella guerra dei Sette Anni (1756–1763) Maria Teresa, che aveva trovato nuovi alleati, giocò il tutto per tutto e perse una guerra, per così dire vinta in partenza. Tra le grandi vittorie austriache vanno menzionate quelle di Kolin (18 giugno 1757) e di Kunersdorf. L'Imperatrice, in una lettera al feldmaresciallo Conte Leopold Daun (1705–1766) definì quello „il giorno della rinascita della Monarchia", e, in quell'occasione, concesse, per la prima volta, l'ordine militare di Maria Teresa. I primi a riceverlo furono Daun e il cognato della stessa Maria Teresa, Carlo di Lorena. E' detto espressamente dall'Imperatrice che „a questo ordine potevano aspirare tutti gli ufficiali superiori, dal grado più alto a quello più basso, compresi i portabandiera, indipendentemente dalla fede, dal rango, dalla nascita e dall'

gion, Rang, Geburt und Dienstjahre im mindesten zurük zu sehen" offen. Nahezu ein Drittel jener Offiziere, die später Theresien-Ritter werden sollten, waren dann auch wirklich bürgerlicher Abstammung.

50 Öffentlicher Einzug der Prinzessin Isabella von Parma als Braut des Erzherzogs Joseph II. in Wien, 1760. Gemälde von Martin van Meytens. (Zeremoniensaal.)

Das Gemälde gehört mit vier weiteren zu einer Serie, die das große Fest der Vermählung der Häuser Habsburg und Bourbon festhalten sollte (Seite 27). Schon während ihres Entstehens waren die Gemälde eine Sensation ob ihres Formats und ihrer Detailtreue. Vor der imaginären Kulisse der Gebäude der heutigen Augustinerstraße stellt Meytens den feierlichen Einzug der Braut des zukünftigen Kaisers dar. Ganz rechts ist eine der beiden Triumphpforten am Ende des Kohlmarktes zu erkennen, die andere, am Stock-im-Eisen-Platz, stellte Meytens auf das große freie Feld, das er zur Darstellung der prunkvollen Auffahrt der 94 sechsspännigen Wagen benötigte. Die silber-blaue Karosse der Braut wird von der Schweizer Garde begleitet, dem Brautwagen voraus fährt der Brautbotschafter Fürst Joseph Wenzel von Liechtenstein im heute noch erhaltenen „Goldenen Wagen". Die Notzeit des Siebenjährigen Krieges hinderte die Kaiserin nicht daran, die Heirat des ältesten Sohnes mit großer Pracht zu feiern – wenn auch zum erheblichen Teil auf Kosten des Fürsten Liechtenstein.
Die Serie der fünf großen Gemälde schmückt den Zeremoniensaal des Schlosses.

51 Wagenburg: Prinzengalawagen und Imperialwagen mit dazugehörigem Gespann.

Das höfische Leben ist ohne Wagen und Schlitten ebensowenig vorstellbar wie ohne Pferde. Es gab sehr viele verschiedene Wagentypen, die den differenzierten Ansprüchen einer weithin luxuriös lebenden Gesellschaft entsprachen. Die beiden wichtigsten Typen von Gala- und Leibwagen waren die ältere Karosse und die jüngere Berline, die zuerst als wendiger Reisewagen gebaut wurde.
Die Schönbrunner Wagenburg bewahrt eine solche Karosse, den Imperialwagen, und mehrere Berlinen, die sogenannten Prinzengalawagen. Der Imperialwagen wurde vermutlich um 1763 als Zeremonienwagen für Kaiser Franz I. (1745–1765) gebaut und anläßlich der Frankfurter Krönung seines Sohnes Joseph II. im Jahr 1764 erstmals verwendet. Dessen Nachfolger in der Kaiserwürde haben ihn als Krönungswagen benützt. Als ranghöchste Staatskarosse des Hauses Österreich blieb er bis zum Jahre 1918 das prunkvolle Schaustück aller großen Feste. Der Wagenkasten ist mit acht allegorischen Gemälden von Franz X. Wagenschön geschmückt, die von üppigen Schnitzereien eingerahmt werden. Ein prachtvolles, rotsamtenes, goldgesticktes Prunkgeschirr für einen Achterzug Kladruber Schimmel läßt den Glanz der kaiserlichen Ausfahrten ahnen.
Die Prinzengalawagen wurden zwischen 1735 und 1750 gebaut, aber noch lange Zeit – einige bis 1916 – bei festlichen Anlässen verwendet.

50 Festive carriage procession of Princess Isabella of Parma entering Vienna as the bride of Archduke Joseph II, in 1760. Painting by Martin van Meytens. (Ceremonial Hall.)

The painting, along with four other ones, was part of a series intended to commemorate the union of the Houses of Hapsburg and Bourbon (page 27). Even before their completion the works were regarded as sensational due to the size of the canvases and the attention to detail. Meytens has depicted the ceremonial procession of the bride of the future emperor in front of the backdrop formed by the then imaginary building facades of today's "Augustinerstrasse". At the far right one of the triumphal arches at the end of the Kohlmarkt can be recognized; the other one, at Stock-im-Eisen Square, was placed by Meytens in the large expanse that he needed for the representation of a procession consisting of ninety-four carriages drawn by teams of six horses. The silver-and-blue state coach of the bride is being accompanied by the "Swiss Guard", preceded by Bridal Ambassador Prince Joseph Wenzel von Liechtenstein in the "Golden Coach" still preserved today. The Seven Years' War did not prevent the Empress from celebrating the marriage of her eldest son in a lavish manner hardly consistent with the rigours of war – even if a large portion of the costs was borne by the Prince of Liechtenstein. This series of paintings adorns the Ceremonial Hall of the palace.

51 Carriage Collection: Princely gala coach and imperial coach with their team.

Courtly life would be as unimaginable without carriages and sleighs as without horses. There were many different models of carriages or coaches corresponding to the differentiated needs of a class accustomed to luxury and extravagance. The two most important types of both gala and private coaches were the traditional caroche and the more recent berlin, which had first been conceived as a travelling carriage.
The Schönbrunn Carriage Collection houses one such caroche, the "Imperialwagen", and several berlins, the so-called "Prinzengalawagen". The "Imperialwagen" is believed to have been built in 1763 as a state coach for Emperor Francis I (1745–1765) and was used for the first time on the occasion of the coronation of his son, Joseph II, in Frankfurt in 1764. It was used as a coronation coach by all later successors to the imperial throne. The pinnacle in the hierachy of the House of Austria's state coaches, it remained until 1918 the lavish showpiece of all grand ceremonies.
The coach body is adorned with eight allegorical paintings by Franz X. Wagenschön, each framed by extravagant carvings. A magnificent harness of red velvet embroidered in gold for a team of eight Kladruber white horses provides an inkling of the splendor of imperial outings.
The "Prinzengalawagen" were built between 1735 and 1750 but continued to be used, some as late as 1916, for years thereafter on ceremonial occasions.

50   Entrée solenelle de la princesse Isabelle de Parme comme fiancée de l'archiduc Joseph II, à Vienne en 1760. Peinture de Martin van Meytens. (Salle des cérémonies.)

Le tableau fait partie d'une série de quatre autres qui devaient fixer par l'image la grande fête de l'alliance entre les maisons de Habsbourg et de Bourbon (page 27). Meytens représente l'entrée solennelle de la fiancée du futur empereur. Tout à droite, on reconnaît l'une des deux portes triomphales à l'extrémité du Kohlmarkt; l'autre, à la place Stock-im-Eisen, fut placée par Meytens sur le grand champ libre dont il avait besoin pour représenter le magnifique défilé des 94 carrosses. Le carrosse bleu et argent de la fiancée est accompagnée par la garde Suisse; le carrosse du fiancé est précédé par le „carrosse doré" qui existe encore aujourd'hui du prince Joseph Wenzel de Liechtenstein, l'ambassadeur de la fiancée. En dépit de l'époque de crise de la guerre de Sept ans, l'impératrice ne voulut pas renoncer à fêter le mariage de son fils aîné avec une pompe qui nétait que difficilement conciliable avec la gravité de la situation – même si une considérable partie des frais était payée par le prince de Liechtenstein. La série des cinq grands tableaux orne la salle des cérémonies du château.

51   Musée des voitures: Les carrosses princiers de gala et le carrosse impérial avec son attelage.

On ne peut se représenter la vie à la cour sans carrosses, sans traineaux ou sans chevaux. Il y avait de très nombreux types différents de carrosses. Les deux types les plus importants pour les carrosses de gala et les voitures personnelles étaient l'ancien carrosse et la berline plus nouvelle qui fut d'abord construite comme luxueuse voiture de voyage.
Le Musée des Voitures de Schönbrunn possède un tel carrosse, le carrosse impérial et plusieurs berlines, dites carrosses princiers de gala. Le carrosse impérial a été probablement construit vers 1763 comme carrosse de cérémonie pour l'empereur François Ier (1745–1765) et employé pour la première fois à l'occasion du couronnement de son fils Joseph II à Francfort en 1764. Il servit de carrosse du couronnement à ses successeurs impériaux. Il resta jusqu'en 1918 un magnifique objet de curiosité dans toutes les grandes fêtes; c'était „le carrosse officiel" de la maison d'Autriche. Les parois de la voiture sont ornées de huit peintures allégoriques de Franz X. Wagenschön, encadrées de riches sculptures en bois. De magnifiques harnais d'apparat en velours rouge brodé d'or pour un attelage de huit chevaux pommelés de Kladruby nous laisse pressentir l'éclat des sorties en carrosse impériales. Les carrosses princiers de gala ont été construits entre 1735 et 1750 mais employés encore très longtemps – certains jusqu'en 1916 – dans les occasions solennelles.

52   Marie-Thérèse à la première investiture de l'ordre de Saint-Etienne le 6 mai 1764. Peinture de Martin van Meytens. (Salon du carrousel.)

Jusqu'au 18ème siècle, on ne connaissait aucun ordre du mérite qu'il fut militaire ou civil. C'est Marie-Thérèse qui, en fondant l'ordre militaire qui porte son nom en 1757, a créé le premier ordre du mérite militaire (page 49) qui pouvait être aussi décerné à des personnes d'origine roturière. Sept ans plus tard, à l'occasion du couronnement de son fils Joseph en tant qu'empereur Romain germanique, elle

anzianità di servizio". Quasi un terzo di quegli ufficiali che, in seguito, sarebbero diventati cavalieri di Maria Teresa, erano di origine borghese.

50   Ingresso ufficiale a Vienna della Principessa Isabella di Parma, sposa dell'Arciduca Giuseppe II (1760). Dipinto di Martin van Meytens. (Sala delle cerimonie.)

Questo dipinto, insieme ad altri quattro, appartiene alla serie celebrativa del matrimonio tra la casa asburgica e quella dei Borboni (pag. 27). Subito questi dipinti furono considerati degli avvenimenti pittorici eccezionali per il loro formato e la loro fedeltà. Da sfondo fa una visione, immaginaria, dei palazzi della Augustinerstrasse, attraverso la quale passerebbe, secondo Meytens, il regale corteo della sposa del futuro Imperatore. A destra si nota uno dei due archi di trionfo in fondo al Kohlmarkt; l'altro, che si trovava sulla piazza Stock-im-Eisen, fu collocato in mezzo alla campagna in quanto l'artista aveva bisogno di molto spazio per poter raffigurare opportunamente il corteo, cosituito da novantaquattro carrozze trainate, ciascuna, da sei cavalli.
La carrozza della sposa, di colore azzurro-argento, è scortata dalle guardie svizzere; è preceduta dall'Ambasciatore, Principe Giuseppe Wenzel di Liechtenstein, che aveva preso posto nella carrozza dorata, ancor oggi conservata. Nonostante fossero tempi duri (imperversava la guerra dei Sette Anni), l'Imperatrice non esitò a festeggiare il matrimonio del figlio maggiore con una pompa forse un po' eccessiva, dato il delicato momento politico. Va aggiunto che riuscì a far pagare la maggior parte delle spese sostenute al Principe di Liechtenstein. La serie dei cinque grandi quadri ornano la sala delle cerimonie del castello.

51   Museo delle carrozze: Carrozze principesche di gala e carrozze imperiale con pariglia di cavalli.

La vita di corte non è immaginabile senza carrozze e senza slitte e, tanto meno, senza cavalli. C'erano molti tipi di carrozze, per ogni esigenza di una società che viveva in modo lussuoso. I tipi più importanti erano la carrozza, di vecchia data, e la berlina, di invenzione più recente che, in quanto più maneggevole, in origine serviva solo come carrozza da viaggio. Il museo delle carrozze (Wagenburg) di Schönbrunn accoglie la carrozza, detta imperiale, e diverse berline, dette anche carrozze principesche di gala. La carrozza imperiale fu costruita probabilmente attorno al 1763 per l'Imperatore Francesco I (1745–1765) e fu usata, per la prima volta, nel 1764, in occasione dell'incoronazione, a Francoforte, di suo figlio Giuseppe II. Successivi Imperatori la useranno sempre in occasione della loro incoronazione. La carrozza imperiale rimase fino al 1918 il pezzo più lussuoso della Casa d'Austria, durante le grandi feste ufficiali. La cassa della carrozza è decorata con otto dipinti allegorici, opera di Francesco X. Wagenschön, cui fanno da cornice ricchi lavori di intaglio. I finimenti sontuosi, in velluto rosso, ricamati in oro per un tiro di otto cavalli bianchi „Kladruber", ci danno un'idea dello splendore delle gite imperiali. Le carrozze principesche di gala furono costruite tra il 1735 e il 1750, furono usate a lungo, alcune fino al 1916, in occasioni solenni.

52   Maria Theresia bei der ersten Verleihung des
St.-Stephans-Ordens am 6. Mai 1764.
Gemälde von Martin van Meytens. (Karussellzimmer.)

Bis zum 18. Jahrhundert kannte man keine militärischen oder zivilen Verdienstorden. Maria Theresia hat durch die Stiftung des nach ihr benannten Militär-Maria-Theresien-Ordens im Jahre 1757 den ersten militärischen Verdienstorden geschaffen (Seite 49), der überdies auch an Nichtadelige verliehen werden konnte. Sieben Jahre später hat sie anläßlich der Krönung ihres Sohnes Joseph zum Römisch-deutschen Kaiser auch einen zivilen Verdienstorden ins Leben gerufen, der nach König Stephan, dem heiligen Landespatron Ungarns, benannt wurde. Der Orden war allerdings noch in traditioneller Weise als Vereinigung gleichgestellter und gleichgesinnter Männer organisiert, mit Ordensstatuten, Ordensfunktionären und festlichem Ordenskostüm, das natürlich in den ungarischen Landesfarben rot-weiß-grün gehalten war.
Auf dem Gemälde, das aus der Werkstatt Meytens' stammt, ist die feierliche erste Promotion in der Großen Anticamera der Wiener Hofburg am 6. Mai 1764 dargestellt. Maria Theresia zeichnete als Königin von Ungarn vier Männer mit dem Großkreuz aus: nach dem ungarischen Primas Erzbischof Franz Barkóczy von Szala, dem ungarischen Palatin Graf Ludwig Ernst Batthyány und dem ungarischen Hofkanzler Graf Franz Esterházy erhält als einziger Nichtungar Graf Karl Friedrich Hatzfeld, Präsident der Hofkammer, das Großkreuz des Ordens. Kaiser Franz Stephan war an diesem Tag, der ganz der „ungarischen Reichshälfte" gehörte, im Zeremoniell gar nicht unterzubringen, weshalb er auf einem eigens errichteten Balkon inkognito zusehen mußte.

52   Damenkarussell des Wiener Hofes in der
Winterreitschule der Hofburg am 2. Jänner 1743.
Gemälde von Martin van Meytens. (Karussellzimmer.)

Im Verlauf des ersten Schlesischen Krieges hatten die vereinigten bayerischen, französischen und sächsischen Truppen im November 1741 Böhmen erobert und Prag besetzt. Maria Theresias Erbe war in höchster Gefahr, die Krone Böhmens trug bereits ein feindlicher Wittelsbacher, Kurfürst Karl Albrecht von Bayern. Im nächsten Jahr sollte er sogar zum Kaiser gekrönt werden! Nach solchen Demütigungen mußten die Siege, die die Österreicher in Bayern und Böhmen im Laufe des Jahres 1742 erfochten, das Herz Maria Theresias höher schlagen lassen. Als im Juli sogar mit der Belagerung Prags begonnen wurde, überlegte man in Wien bereits, wie der bevorstehende Sieg zu feiern wäre. Wochenlang probte Maria Theresia mit ihren Damen ein Karussell, das nach dem Abzug der Feinde aus Prag auch tatsächlich mit jener Mischung von Pracht und Grazie aufgeführt wurde, die für das Rokoko charakteristisch ist. In aller Eile hatte man reich verzierte Muschelwägelchen angefertigt, von denen einer in der Schönbrunner Wagenburg erhalten ist.
Vier Quadrillen wurden aufgestellt, zwei gerittene mit Maria Theresia an der Spitze, und zwei gefahrene, mit Maria Theresias Schwester Maria Anna, geführt vom Prinzen Joseph von Sachsen-Hilburghausen im ersten Wagen. Bei der Aufführung galt es, seine Geschicklichkeit im Pistolenschießen, Pfeilwerfen, Lanzenstechen und vor allem im Reiten zu zeigen. Es fehlte nicht an spitzen Bemerkungen, daß der sportliche Ehrgeiz der Herrscherin dazu führte, daß „alle Weiber die Rage haben ihr nach zu ammen" und daß die „Frauen und

52   Maria Theresa awarding the Order of St. Stephen's for
the first time on 6 May, 1764.
Painting by Martin van Meytens. (Carousel Room.)

Until the eighteenth century there were neither military nor civilian decorations. Maria Theresa founded the Military Order of Maria Theresa named after her in 1757 (page 49), which could be awarded to commoners also. Seven years later, on the occasion of the investiture of her son Joseph as Holy Roman Emperor, she founded a civilian order named after King Stephen, the patron saint of Hungary. The order was organised along traditional lines as an association of men of common rank and outlook – with its own statutes, functionaries, and ceremonial costumes in the red, white, and green colours of Hungary. The painting, by the school of Meytens, depicts the first conferment of the decoration on 6th May, 1764 in the Large Antechamber of the Hofburg palace. Maria Theresa, as Queen of Hungary, distinguished four men with the Grand Cross: Primate Archbishop Franz Barkóczy von Szala; Count Palatine Ludwig Ernst Batthyány; the Hungarian Chancellor, Count Franz Esterházy; and Count Karl Friedrich Hatzfeld, President of the Exchequer, who was the only non-Hungarian to receive the award. Emperor Francis could not be included in the ceremony devoted entirely to the Hungarian half of the empire, for which reason he is shown as incognito spectator on a balcony erected especially for the occasion.

52   The Ladies' Carousel at the Court of Vienna in the
Winter Riding School of the Hofburg, on 2 January, 1743.
Painting by Martin van Meytens. (Carousel Room.)

In the course of the first Silesian War, the allied troops of Bavaria, France, and Saxony conquered Bohemia in 1741 and occupied Prague. Maria Theresa's hereditary dominion was in jeopardy; the Bohemian crown already adorned the head of a Wittelsbach enemy, Prince Elector Karl Albrecht of Bavaria. In a year he even intended to be crowned Emperor! After such humiliations, the Austrian victories won in Bavaria and Bohemia in 1742 must have relieved Maria Theresa immensely. When the siege of Prague was begun in July, it was already being deliberated in Vienna how best to celebrate the foreseeable victory. For weeks Maria Theresa and the ladies of the court rehearsed a carousel which, when Austria's enemies abandoned Prague, was actually performed with that mixture of grace and pomp characteristic of the rococo. In all haste special lavishly decorated shell-like carriages had been constructed, one of which is preserved in the Schönbrunn Carriage Collection. Of the four quadrilles performed, two were ridden, with Maria Theresa at the fore, and two driven, with Maria Theresa's sister, Maria Anna, being driven by Prince Joseph von Sachsen-Hilburghausen in the first carriage. The performance was intended to demonstrate proficiency in pistol shooting, spear throwing, jousting and, above all, riding. There was no dearth of sarcastic remarks to the effect that the sporting ambitions of their monarch would "inflame the passions of all women to imitate her", or that the "ladies and maidens" were seated on their horses "after the fashion of men" instead of in a more befitting, "womanly" manner.
Maria Theresa's mother, the widowed Empress Elisabeth Christine, and her husband, Grand Duke Francis Stephen of Tuscany, are seated in the box beneath the picture of Emperor Charles VI on horseback, which still hangs there today.

fonda également un ordre du mérite civil qui reçut son nom du saint patron de la Hongrie, le roi Etienne. Toutefois, l'ordre était encore organisé de manière traditionelle en tant que association d'hommes égaux et ayant les mêmes opinions, avec les statuts de l'ordre, les fonctionnaires de l'ordre et un costume solonnel de l'ordre dont les couleurs étaient naturellement celles de la Hongrie: rouge, blanc, vert.

Le tableau de l'atelier de Meytens représente la première investiture solennelle du 6 mai 1764 dans la grande antichambre de la Hofburg à Vienne. En tant que reine de Hongrie, Marie-Thérèse décora quatre hommes de la grand'croix: après le primat hongrois, l'archevêque Franz Barkóczy von Szala, le palatin hongrois, le comte Ludwig Ernst Batthyány et le chancelier hongrois de la cour, le comte Franz Esterházy, le comte Karl Friedrich Hatzfeld, président de la chambre aulique des comptes, est le seul non hongrois à recevoir la grand'croix de l'ordre. Ce jour-là qui appartenait tout entier à la „moitié hongroise du royaume", le protocole n'avait pas réussi à trouver une place à l'empereur François pour la cérémonie; c'est pourquoi, il dut y assister incognito d'un balcon érigé exprès pour lui.

52   Carrousel des dames de la Cour de Vienne au Manège d'hiver de la Hofburg le 2 janvier 1743. Peinture de Martin van Meytens. (Salon du carrousel.)

Au cours de la première guerre de Silésie, les troupes bavaroises, françaises et saxonnes réunies avaient conquis la Bohême en novembre 1741 et occupé Prague. L'héritage de Marie-Thérèse était en grand danger. Un ennemi Wittelsbach, le prince électeur Charles-Albert de Bavière portrait déjà la couronne de Bohême. L'année suivante, il devait même être couronné empereur! Apres de telles humiliations, les victoires que les Autrichiens remportèrent en Bavière et en Bohême au cours de l'année 1742 devaient enthousiasmer Marie-Thérèse. Lorsqu'en juillet le siège de Prague commença, on se demandait déjà à Vienne comment on pourrait fêter la victoire imminente. Pendant des semaines, Marie-Thérèse et ses dames répétèrent un carrousel qui fut finalement représenté après l'évacuation de Prague par les ennemis avec ce mélange de somptuosité et de grâce qui est caractéristique du rococo. On avait fabriqué en toute hâte des petites voitures richement ornées en forme de conque; on peut voir l'une d'elles au Musée des Voitures de Schönbrunn. On avait formé quatre quadrilles, deux à cheval avec Marie-Thérèse en tête et deux en voiture avec Marie-Anne la sœur de Marie-Thérèse, menés par le prince Joseph de Saxe-Hilburghausen dans la première voiture. Au cours de la représentation, il fallait faire preuve d'adresse dans le tir au pistolet, le lancer de flèches, en joute et surtout en équitation. Il ne manqua pas de remarques acerbes au sujet de l'ambition sportive de la souveraine qui menait à ce que „toutes les femmes aient la rage de l'imiter" et que les „femmes et jeunes filles chevauchaient comme des hommes" et non de manière „féminine". La mère de Marie-Thérèse, l'impératrice veuve Elisabeth-Christine, et son époux, le grand-duc François de Toscane étaient assis dans les loges sous le portrait équestre de l'empereur Charles VI qui, aujourd'hui encore, est suspendu à cet endroit.

52   Maria Teresa durante il primo solenne conferimento dell'ordine civile di Santo Stefano, il 6 maggio 1764. Dipinto di Martin van Meytens. (Stanza del carosello.)

Fino al XVIII secolo non si conoscevano gli ordini militari o civili. Si deve a Maria Terese l'istituzione, nel 1757, del primo ordine militare, chiamato appunto „ordine militare di Maria Teresa" (pag. 49). Questo poteva essere conferito anche a persone non nobili. Sette anni più tardi Maria Teresa istituí anche un ordine civile in occasione dell'incoronazione di suo figlio Giuseppe a Imperatore del Sacro romano impero germanico. Questo ordine prese il nome dal Re Stefano, santo patrono dell'Ungheria. L'ordine era organizzato in modo tradizionale e cioé era conferito a persone dello stesso livello sociale, affini per idee. Vi erano degli statuti, dei funzionari, un abito particolare da indossare nelle occasioni ufficiali, che aveva naturalmente i colori nazionali, rosso, bianco, e verde. Nel dipinto, proveniente dalla scuola di Meytens, è rappresentato il primo solenne conferimento di questo ordine, avvenuto il 6 maggio 1764 nella grande „Anticamera" dell'Hofburg viennese. Maria Teresa, regina d'Ungheria, insignisce quattro uomini della grande croce. Oltre al primate ungherese, Arcivescovo Francesco Barkóczy von Szala, al Conte palatino ungherese Ludovico Ernesto Batthyány, e al cancelliere della corte ungherese, conte Esterházy, il Conte Carlo Federico Hatzfeld, presidente della camera di corte, unico personaggio non ungherese, riceve l'ambita onorificienza.

Dal punto di vista del cerimoniale era molto difficile poter date una collocazione adeguata all'Imperatore Francesco Stefano che rappresentava „la metà ungherese" del regno di Maria Teresa. Si costruí un apposito balcone dal quale l'Imperatore potesse seguire, in incognito, la cerimonia.

52   Corteo a cavallo delle dame della Corte imperiale viennese presso la Scuola invernale d'equitazione nella Hofburg, il 2 gennaio 1743. Dipinto di Martin van Meytens. (Stanza del carosello.)

Durante la prima guerra slesiana le truppe alleate bavaresi, francesi e sassoni avevano conquistato, nel novembre 1741, la Boemia ed avevano occupato Praga. I territori ereditati da Maria Teresa correvano un grandissimo pericolo. La corona di Boemia era caduta nelle mani del Principe elettorale Carlo Albrecht di Bavaria, della Casa Wittelsbach, grande nemico dell'Imperatrice d'Austria.

L'anno seguente questi sarebbe stato persino incoronato imperatore! Dopo queste umiliazioni, le vittorie degli Austriaci in Bavaria e in Boemia, ottenute gloriosamente nel 1742, avevano dato nuovo coraggio a Maria Teresa. Nel mese di luglio, quando cominciò l'assedio di Praga, a Vienna si valutò la possibilità di festeggiare l'imminente vittoria. Per intere settimane Maria Teresa fece le prove con le sue dame, per realizzare un corteo a cavallo, che ebbe poi luogo, in effetti, dopo il ritiro del nemico da Praga. L'avvenimento fu festeggiato con quello sfarzo e quella grazia che sono così caratteristici del Rococò. In tutta fretta furono costruite delle carrozzelle a forma di conchiglia; se ne può ammirare ancora oggi una nel museo delle carrozze di Schönbrunn (Wagenburg).

Furono organizzate quattro quadriglie. In due i partecipanti erano a cavallo, con intesta Maria Teresa; nella altre due, invece, le persone erano in carrozza e, nella prima di queste, guidata dal Principe Giuseppe von Sachsen-Hilburghausen, si trovava Maria Anna,

Freilen (Fräulein) auf Männer-Art placiret" waren, und nicht „weiberisch" ritten.

In der Loge sitzen die verwitwete Kaiserin Elisabeth Christine, die Mutter Maria Theresias, und deren Gemahl, Großherzog Franz Stephan von Toskana, unter dem Reiterbildnis Kaiser Karls VI. Es hängt noch heute an dieser Stelle.

54/55   Das Runde Chinesische Zimmer.

Das Runde und das Ovale Chinesische Zimmer schmiegen sich zu beiden Seiten der Kleinen Galerie in die Rundungen des Mittelrisalits. Porzellan und Lackarbeiten, die kostbaren ostasiatischen Lieblinge der fürstlichen Wohnkultur des 18. Jahrhunderts, sind in diesen beiden intimen Räumen zu einer bezaubernden Einheit mit der europäischen Rokokodekoration verschmolzen. In die weiße Holzvertäfelung (Boiserie) sind die schwarz-goldenen Laque-Tafeln eingelassen. Aus den Stegen und Ornamenten ihrer vergoldeten Umrahmungen wachsen kleine Konsolen, auf denen weiß-blaues Porzellan steht. Große japanische Porzellanvasen mit herrlichem blau-rotem Dekor stehen auf dem eingelegten Fußboden. Die Rocaillen, Blumenranken und Zweige der Rahmungen von Tafeln und Spiegeln wiederholen sich im Fries, der flachen Kuppel. Die emaillierten Beleuchtungskörper sind eine Wiener Arbeit.

Zum westlichen, runden Kabinett gab es zu Maria Theresias Zeit einen Speisenaufzug, um unbelauscht Gespräche führen zu können. Nach solchen kleinen Konferenzen blieb die Kaiserin gerne beim Kartenspiel sitzen. Die hohen Einsätze, um die sie vor allem beim „Pharao" spielte, wurden sogar vom Kaiser kritisiert.

56/57   Das Vieux-Laque-Zimmer mit den Bildnissen von Batoni und Maron.

Auch im Vieux-Laque-Zimmer sind ostasiatische Lacktafeln in die dunkelbraune Nußholzvertäfelung eingesetzt. Bis zur Decke reichen die schweren Dekorationen und auch in den vergoldeten Stuck-Kartuschen und in den Festons, die zwischen diesen zu hängen scheinen, sind Lacktafeln oder kleine runde Ausschnitte daraus eingefügt. Den Entwurf für diese ebenso einheitliche wie prächtige Raumgestaltung lieferte der französische Architekt Isidor Canevale im Jahre 1770, unmittelbar nachdem die Tafeln um 12.869 Gulden gekauft worden waren. Die Schnitzereien stammen von J. G. Leithner. Der Unterschied zwischen den spielerisch leichten Dekorationen der chinesischen Kabinette sowie der Galerien und den schweren, kompakten Rahmungen, den Kränzen, Maschen und Zöpfen in diesem Raum ist auf den ersten Blick erkennbar. Die Rokokozeit geht ihrem Ende zu.

Von Anfang an war geplant, in drei Wände dieses Raumes qualitätsvolle Familienbilder einzulassen, für die an zwei berühmte Maler der Zeit, Pompeo Batoni und Anton von Maron, die Aufträge ergangen waren. Das Porträt des Stammvaters des Hauses Habsburg-Lothringen, Kaiser Franz I. Stephan, wurde von Pompeo Batoni im Jahre 1772 (also posthum) in Rom gemalt. Der Künstler war ein Freund und Gesinnungsgenosse Winckelmanns und einer der gefeiertesten Maler des Klassizismus. Sein Doppelbild der Söhne Joseph und Leopold (Seite 66) hatte 1769 bei Maria Theresia so große Begeisterung hervorgerufen, daß sie eine zweite Fassung für Schönbrunn und auch ein Porträt des 1765 verstorbenen Kaisers in Auftrag gab.

54/55   The Round Chinese Room.

The Oval and the Round Chinese Room are nestled against either side of the Small Gallery in the curved portions of the middle projection. Here fine porcelain and lacquer-work, the two costly East Asian favourites of princely eighteenth century furnishings, have been blended with European rococo decorations into a bewitching harmony. The black-and-gold lacquer panels are set into the white woodwork. From the fillets and gilt ornamentation project small consoles, atop which small blue-and-white porcelain vases are placed. Large Japanese vases of blue-and-red design grace the parquet floor. The rocailles, flower tendrils and branches framing the panels and mirrors are repeated in the frieze extending along the base of the flat cupola.

In Maria Theresa's time there was a service-lift to the round room on the western side, to allow private and undisturbed meals. Following such private conferences, the Empress was wont to play cards. Her high stakes, especially when she played "pharao", elicited the criticism of even the Emperor.

56/57   The "Vieux-Laque" Room with the portraits by Batoni and Maron.

In the Vieux-Laque Room, East Asian lacquer panels have been set into the dark brown walnut paneling. The heavy decorations extend all the way to the ceiling, with lacquer panels or small round sections thereof inserted into the stucco cartouches and festoons seemingly suspended between them. These equally uniform and sumptuous decorations were designed by the French architect, Isidor Canevale, in 1770, immediately after the purchase of the panels for 12,869 guldens. The carvings are the work of J. G. Leithner. The difference of the playfully light decorations of the Chinese Rooms and the Galleries to this room's heavy, compact frames, wreathes, bows and plaits is readily apparent. The Rococo was nearing its end.

It had been planned from the beginning to set into three walls of the room high-quality family portraits, for wich two famous contemporary painters, Pomeo Batoni and Anton von Maron, were commissioned. The portrait of the progenitor of the House of Hapsburg-Lorraine, Emperor Francis I, was created posthumously by Pompeo Batoni in Rome in 1772. The artist was a friend and adherent of Winckelmann's, and one of the most celebrated neo-classical painters. His double-portrait of Maria Theresa's sons, Joseph and Leopold (page 66), evinced so much enthusiasm in 1769 that she commissioned a second version for Schönbrunn in addition to a portrait of her husband, who had died in 1765. The decoration of the room could not be completed until the last painting had arrived from Rome in 1773. Maria Theresa paid both artists a total of 8,287 guldens. As examples of early neoclassical art these paintings are in sharp contrast to the richly ornamental decorations of the room and herald the impending change of style.

54/55 Le cabinet chinois rond.

Les cabinets chinois ovale et rond sont situés des deux côtés de la Petite Galerie. La porcelaine et les ouvrages de laque précieux de l'Asie orientale, forment avec la décoration rococo européenne de ces deux pièces intimes un ensemble ravissant. Dans la boiserie blanche on a encastré des plaques de laque noir et or. Des moulures et ornements de leur cadre doré sortent de petites consoles sur lesquelles la porcelaine bleue et blanche est posée. De grands vases de porcelaine japonais au magnifique décor bleu et rouge sont posés à même le parquet en marqueterie. Le lustre et les candélabres sont des ouvrages viennois.

A l'époque de Marie-Thérèse, le cabinet rond de l'ouest disposait d'un monte-plats, ce qui permettait de pouvoir mener des conversations loin des oreilles indiscrètes. Après de telles petites conférences, l'impératrice restait volontiers assise pour jouer aux cartes. Elle jouait gros jeu, surtout au „pharaon", ce qui lui valut même les critiques de l'empereur.

56/57 Le salon Vieux-Laque avec les portraits de Batoni et Maron.

On a également encastré des panneaux de laque d'Asie orientale dans la boiserie en noyer brun foncé du salon Vieux-Laque. C'est l'architecte français Isidore Canevale qui dessina la décoration aussi uniforme que magnifique de ce salon immédiatement après que les panneaux aient été achetés pour 12.689 florins. Les sculptures sur bois sont dûes à J. G. Leithner. On reconnaît du premier coup d'œil la différence entre les décorations légères et enjouées des cabinets chinois de même que des galeries et les encadrements lourds et compacts, les couronnes, les nœuds et les tresses de cette pièce. L'époque rococo tire vers sa fin.

Dès le début, on avait prévu de suspendre sur trois murs de cette pièce de tableaux de famille de qualité qu'on avait commandés à deux peintres célèbres de l'époque, Pompeo Batoni et Anton von Maron. Le portrait du fondateur de la maison de Habsbourg Lorraine, François Ier, a été peint à Rome par Pompeo Batoni en 1772 (donc, il est posthume). L'artiste était un ami de Winckelmann dont il partageait les idées et l'un des peintres les plus fêtés de l'époque néo-classique. Son portrait double des fils de Marie-Thérèse, Joseph et Leopold (page 66) avait provoqué en 1769 un si grand enthousiasme de la part de l'impératrice qu'elle lui commanda une deuxième version pour Schönbrunn et également un portrait de l'empereur mort en 1765. Les travaux de cette pièce ne purent être terminés qu'après l'arrivée de Rome du dernier portrait, donc, au plus tôt, en 1773. Marie-Thérèse avait fait payer aux deux peintres une somme totale de 8.287 florins. Les tableaux forment un contraste sévère avec la magnificence de l'intérieur comme œuvres du début du néo-classique et sont un présage du changement imminent de style.

sorella di Maria Teresa. Era importante mostrare la propria abilità nell'uso della pistola, nel lancio della freccia e dell'asta, ma suprattutto nel cavalcare. Qualcuno, acido, ebbe a osservare: „L'ambizione sportiva dell'Imperatrice spinge le signore a fare altrettanto". E ancora: „Le signore e signorine usano, a cavallo, la posizione maschile e non quella femminile".

Nella loggia, al di sotto del quadro equestre dell'Imperatore Carlo VI, hanno preso posto l'Imperatrice Maria Cristina, ormai vedova, madre di Maria Teresa, e il marito di quest'ultima, Granduca Francesco Stefano di Toscana. Il quadro dell'Imperatore Carlo VI è ancor oggi al medesimo posto.

54/55 Il Salottino cinese rotondo.

Il Salottino cinese ovale e quello rotondo si trovano rispettivamente prima e dopo la piccola galleria, là dove, per via delle scale di accesso centrali, si creano, nell'edifico, due zone tonde. In queste stanze, particolarmente intime, porcellane e lacche, tanto amate dai principi nel XVIII secolo, soprattutto a livello di decorazione di interni, si fondono mirabilmente con il gusto rococò. Nel rivestimento ligneo delle pareti sono inserite delle tavole laccate di colore nero e oro. Dalle cornici dorate che le circondano nascono delle piccole console sulle quali sono posati dei vasi di porcellana bianca e azzurra. Sul pavimento a intarsi poggiano dei grandi vasi di porcellana giapponesi decorati in rosso e blu. Le rocailles, i fiori e i rami che circondano le tavole e gli specchi si ripetono nel fregio della cupola. Le lampade smaltate sono state eseguite a Vienna.

All'epoca di Maria Teresa, un montacarichi portava nella stanza cinese occidentale le vivande direttamente dalla cucina; questo, per poter tenere delle riunioni in tutta calma senza correre il rischio di venir spiati. Dopo tali riunioni l'Imperatrice era solita fare una partita a carte. Soprattutto nel gioco del „Faraone" Maria Teresa puntava molto alto: l'Imperatore criticava severamente questo comportamento della consorte.

56/57 La Stanza vieux-laque con i ritratti di Batoni e Maron.

Anche nella stanza vieux-laque vediamo come delle tavole laccate, provenienti dall'Asia Orientale, siano inserite nel rivestimento di noce scuro delle pareti. La decorazione, indubbiamente pesante, giunge sino al soffitto; le tavole di lacca o piccole parti rotonde, sempre in lacca, si inseriscono tra gli stucchi dorati e i festoni. Il progetto di questo locale, unitario e sontuoso, è dell'architetto francese Isidor Canevale (1770), immediatamente dopo che erano state acquistate queste tavole per 12.869 corone. Gli intagli sono opera di J. G. Leithner. Ci si accorge subito della enorme differenza che esiste tra le decorazioni, delicate e leggere, delle stanze cinesi e delle gallerie e le cornici, le ghirlande, i fiocchi e le trecce che ornano questa stanza. Il Rococò sta finendo. In un primo momento si era pensato di inserire in tre pareti alcuni ritratti di famiglia di eccellente fattura, della cui esecuzione erano stati incaricati due pittori, molto famosi a quei tempi, Pompeo Batoni e Antonio von Maron.

Il ritratto del fondatore della Casa Asburgo-Lorena, l'Imperatore Francesco Stefano I, fu dipinto a Roma nel 1772, dunque postumo, da Pompeo Batoni. Questo artista era amico e seguace di Winckelmann e uno dei pittori più considerati del Classicismo. A lui si deve il dipin-

Die Arbeiten an dem Raum konnten wohl erst abgeschlossen werden, nachdem das letzte der Gemälde aus Rom eingetroffen war, also frühestens 1773. Maria Theresia hat den beiden Malern insgesamt 8287 Gulden ausbezahlen lassen.

58/59 Das Millionenzimmer und die indopersischen Miniaturen.

Die blendende Pracht dieses kleinen Raumes mit den überaus kostbaren indopersischen Miniaturen hat zur Bezeichnung „Millionenzimmer" geführt, die aber nicht historisch verbürgt ist. Das Zimmer war bis nach dem Tode Kaiser Franz' I. ein Spiegelzimmer und wurde danach umgestaltet. Erst seit kurzem weiß man, daß Maria Theresia die edle Holzvertäfelung aus dem Oberen Belvedere hierher übertragen ließ. Wahrscheinlich geschah dies 1767, denn seither lesen wir von einem „Vicatin-Cabinet". Dieser Name leitet sich vom rostbraunen Vegetin- oder Rosenholz her. Es ist von einem goldflimmernden Netz überzogen, das die Boiserie durch unterbrochene senkrechte Linien in Felder unterteilt, in denen meist drei Rocaille-Rahmen übereinander angeordnet sind. Auch die Türen, die einander gegenüberliegenden Spiegel, der Kamin und eine originelle, flache Attrappe einer Kommode sind virtuos in dieses goldene Linienspiel eingebunden. Über die Wandvertäfelung ist ein gemaltes Gitterwerk von Wandmalereien unterbrochen, die stilistisch und thematisch zu den Miniaturen in der Boiserie passen. In den Rahmen sehen diese wie Bilder aus, bei näherer Betrachtung erkennt man aber, daß mehrere nicht zusammengehörige Blätter oft recht willkürlich angeordnet wurden.

Maria Theresia benützte diesen Raum, der sich in seiner barocken Farbigkeit von den anderen Schönbrunner Zimmern unterscheidet, als Audienz- und Konferenzzimmer. Kaiser Franz Joseph stellte ihn regelmäßig seinen Gästen zur Verfügung.

60 Der Blaue oder Chinesische Salon.

Dieser Salon liegt zwischen dem großen Zeremoniensaal und dem intimen Vieux-Laque-Zimmer und entspricht dem Spiegelzimmer des Westflügels. Auch er wurde nach dem Tode Kaiser Franz' I., dem er als Ratstube und Audienzraum gedient hatte, verändert. Er ist aber wohl erst im 19. Jahrhundert, zusammen mit anderen Räumen dieses Traktes mit den chinesischen Tapeten verkleidet worden, die ihm seinen Namen gegeben haben. Auf den einzelnen Bahnen folgen regelmäßig drei Motive übereinander: ein kleines ovales und ein größeres, rechteckiges, blaues Feld mit Szenen aus dem Alltag der Chinesen, darüber ein Korb mit Blumen; Schmetterlinge, Vögel und Blumen sind über den freien Grund der Tapete verstreut. Das Mobiliar des Raumes ist kostbar. Die Platten der Tische sind mit Florentiner Steinmosaik belegt, an der Wand stehen Lackmöbel. Die Lacktafeln wurden oft schon in China zu Kabinettschränken, Kästchen oder Paravents nach europäischem Geschmack für den Export verarbeitet. Seit dem Beginn des 18. Jahrhunderts wurde die Lackkunst in Europa (wie das Porzellan) erfolgreich nachgeahmt und erreichte ihre Blüte in London, Paris, Venedig und Dresden; vielfach wurden die Möbel in Europa gezimmert, in Asien lackiert und wieder zurücktransportiert.

In diesem Raum erklärte Kaiser Karl am 11. November 1918 seinen Verzicht auf die Mitwirkung an der Regierung Österreich-Ungarns.

58/59 The "Million Gulden Room" with its Indo-Persian miniatures.

The overwhelming splendour of this small room of costly Indo-Persian miniatures has led to this name which can, however not be verified historically. The Million Gulden Room was a room of mirrors until it was re-furnished after the death of Emperor Francis I. Only recently did it become known that Maria Theresa had the precious wood paneling transferred here from the Upper Belvedere. This probably took place in 1767, for since then there is mention of a "Vicatin Cabinet". The name was derived from a rust-colored species of rosewood. The walls of the room are covered with a gilt web that divides the woodwork (Boiserie) into vertical strips usually with three rocaille ornaments placed one above the other. Even the doors, the mirrors facing each other, the fireplace, and the mock front of a commode are masterfully incorporated into the play of golden lines. Above the wall paneling the painted latticework ist interrupted by small pictures that match the miniatures in the rocailles, both stylistically and thematically. Within their gilt frames they, too, appear to be paintings, but upon closer inspection one discovers that several unrelated sheets were often rather whimsically placed next to one another.

Maria Theresa used this room, which distinguishes itself from other rooms of the palace by virtue of its colourfulness, as an audience and conference room. Emperor Francis Joseph regularly placed it at the disposal of his guests.

60 The Blue or Chinese Drawing-Room.

This drawing-room, located between the large Ceremonial Hall and the intimate Vieux-Laque Room, is the counterpart to the Room of Mirrors in the west wing. Used by Emperor Francis I as a council chamber and audience room, it, too, was re-decorated after his death. The Chinese wall hangings that have given the room its name were first put up in the nineteenth century, both in this room and in others of this wing. Three motifs are arranged above one another at regular intervals within each vertical strip: a small oval and a larger rectangular blue background with depictions of scenes from everyday Chinese life; above them a basket with flowers. Butterflies, flowers, and birds are scattered over the remaining surface of the wall hanging. The room's furniture is valuable. The table tops are inlaid with Florentine marble mosaic; lacquered furniture stands against the wall. Often lacquered panels were assembled already in China into cabinets, chests, or folding screens, for export to Europe. The art of lacquering was successfully copied in Europe since the beginning of the eigtheenth century and thrived especially in London, Paris, Venice, and Dresden. In many cases, furniture built in Europe was lacquered in Asia before being shipped back to Europe.

In this room Emperor Charles declared his resignation from participation in the Austro-Hungarian government on 11 November, 1918.

61 The Porcelain Room with the medallion of Archduchess Maria Christine.

The most remarkable thing about the Schönbrunn state rooms is the role the imperial family played in designing and furnishing them. The artistic ornamentation of the rooms does not serve merely to depict allegorically the usual virtues of monarchs or to glorify the history of the dynasty, or even simply to demonstrate power and

58/59 Le salon des Millions et les miniatures indo-persanes.

La splendeur aveuglante de cette petite pièce aux miniatures indo-persanes extrêment précieuses a été la raison pour laquelle on lui a donné le nom de „salon des Millions", nom qui n'est pas historiquement exact. La pièce fut jusqu'après la mort de l'empereur François Ier un salon de glaces et subit ensuite des remaniements. Les boiseries sont couvertes d'un réseau d'or étincelant qui les partagent en panneaux par des lignes verticales discontinues; généralement, on a encastré dans ces panneaux trois cadres en rocaille l'un au-dessus de l'autre. Les portes, les glaces se faisant face, la cheminée et une commode plate attrappe sont reliées aec virtuosité pour former un jeu doré de lignes. Au dessous de la boiserie, un treillage peint est interrompu de peintures murales qui s'accordent des points de vue style et thème avec les miniatures encastrées dans la boiserie. Dans leur cadre, celles ci ont l'air de tableaux; mais, si on les regarde de plus près, on reconnait que plusieurs gravures n'allant pas ensemble sont placées bien arbitrairement.
Marie-Thérèse utilisait cette pièce qui se distingue des autres pièces de Schönbrunn par ses couleurs baroques comme salle d'audience et de conférence. L'empereur François-Joseph la mettait régulièrement à la disposition de ses hôtes.

60 Le salon bleu ou salon chinois.

Il a été remanié après la mort de l'empereur François Ier à qui il avait servi de salle du conseil et de salle d'audience. Mais ce n'est qu'au 19 ème siècle qu'on y posa ainsi que dans d'autres pièces de cette aile des papiers peints chinois qui lui ont donné son nom. Trois motifs l'un au-dessus de l'autre se suivent régulièrement sur les panneaux: un petit champ ovale, un champ rectangulaire plus grand, bleu, avec des scènes de la vie chinoise quotidienne et au-dessus, un corbeille avec des fleurs; des papillons, des oiseaux et des fleurs sont disséminés sur le fond libre du papier peint. Les dessus des tables sont incrustés d'une mosaïque de pierres florentines; des meubles de laque se dressent contre le mur. Les panneaux de laque ont souvent été travaillés en Chine en cabinets, petites armoires ou paravents d'après le goût européen pour l'exportation. Depuis le début du 18 ème siècle l'art du laque a souvent été imité avec succès en Europe (comme la porcelaine) et atteignit son apogée à Londres, Paris, Venise et Dresde; souvent, les meubles furent fabriqués en Europe, laqués en Asie et retransportés en Europe.
Dans ce salon l'empereur Charles s'est désisté de la participation au gouvernement de l'Autriche-Hongrie le 11 novembre 1918.

61 Le salon des Porcelaines avec le médaillon de l'archiduchesse Marie-Christine.

Ce qu'il y a de plus remarquable dans les salles d'apparat de Schönbrunn, c'est que la famille impériale ait contribué à compléter et à faire la décoration intérieure. L'ornementation artistique de ces pièces ne sert pas à représenter allégoriquement les vertus bien connues des souverains ni à glorifier l'histoire de la dynastie, ni seulement à faire montre de leur puissance et de leur richesse, mais au contraire elle présente l'déal familial, pour ne pas dire l'idylle familiale de la „première mère" de l'empire.
Le salon des Porcelaines tient son nom des guirlandes en bois sculpté peintes bleu et blanc sur les murs de la pièce et qui imitent la porce-

to, ultimato nel 1769, che ritraeva Giuseppe e Leopoldo (pag. 66). Tale dipinto piacque a tal punto a Maria Teresa che ne commissionò un secondo per Schönbrunn; incaricò dunque l'artista italiano di fare un ritratto dell'Imperatore, morto nel 1765.
In questo locale si poterono ultimare i lavori solo dopo l'arrivo dell'ultimo quadro da Roma, dunque non prima del 1773.

58/59 La Stanza dei milioni e le miniature indopersiane.

Sebbene non sia storicamente dimostrato, questa piccola stanza deve il suo soprannome, „stanza dei milioni", allo sfavillante splendore che la caratterizza (si notino le preziose miniature indopersiane). Fino alla morte dell'Imperatore Francesco I questa era una stanza degli specchi. Solo in seguito fu trasformata. Da studi recenti sappiamo che Maria Teresa utilizzò per il locale il rivestimento ligneo del Belvedere Superiore. Probabilmente nel 1767 fece portare a Schönbrunn le tavole da Vienna: in pari data infatti sentiamo parlare di un „Vicatin-Cabinet". La parola „vicatin" è tratta dal legno „vegetin" o legno di rosa. E' ricoperto di una rete dorata che, con linee verticali, qua e là interrotte, suddivide il legno in campi nei quali sono inserite, l'una sopra l'altra, tre cornici rocaille. Perfettamente adatto a questo gioco di linee dorate sono le porte, gli specchi, che sono collocati l'uno di fronte all'altro, il camino e un finto comò di cui è presente solo la parte anteriore. Al di sopra del rivestimento ligneo delle pareti vi è una grata dipinta, interrotta da affreschi che ben si adattano, sia per lo stile che per il tema, alle miniature inserite nella boiserie. Queste, grazie anche al modo con cui sono incorniciate, sembrano dei veri e propri quadri. Se le si osserva più da vicino si nota che sono state ordinate in modo piuttosto arbitrario.
Maria Teresa utilizzava questa stanza che, per la sua barocca vanità di colori, si differenzia sensibilmente da tante altre stanze del Castello, per le udienze o per le riunioni. L'Imperatore Francesco Giuseppe la metteva invece a disposizione dei propri ospiti.

60 Il Salone azzurro o cinese.

Questo salone si trova tra la grande sala delle cerimonie e la stanza vieux-laque, tanto intima. Come posizione corrisponde alla stanza degli specchi dell'ala ovest. Fu trasformato dopo la morte dell' Imperatore Francesco I che si serviva di questo salone per le udienze e per le riunioni. Solo verso il 1800, fu rivestito, insieme ad altri locali di questa ala, con tappeti cinesi; a questo fatto deve il proprio nome. Tre sono i motivi che si susseguono regolarmente: su campo azzurro, piccolo e ovale o più grande e rettangolare, sono rappresentate delle scene della vita quotidiana cinese. Queste sono sormontate da un cesto di fiori, al di sopra del quale, liberi, sulla tappezzeria, si possono ammirare degli uccelli e delle farfalle e ancora dei fiori. Preziosissimi sono i mobili: le superfici dei tavoli sono intarsiate con mosaici fiorentini, alla parete poggiano mobili di lacca. Le tavole di lacca furono spesso utilizzate, in Cina, per costruire armadietti, mobili o paraventi, secondo il gusto europeo, in quanto avevano come fine quello dell'esportazione. A partire dai primi anni del 1700 in Europa si imitò, con successo, l'arte della lacca e della porcellana. Essa fiorì a Londra, Parigi, Venezia e Dresda. Spesso i mobili venivano costruiti in Europa, inviati in Asia per la laccatura e ritrasportati in Europa. L'11 novembre del 1918 in questa stanza l'imperatore Carlo dichiarava la sua rinuncia a partecipare al governo.

61   Das Porzellanzimmer mit dem Medaillon der Erzherzogin Maria Christine.

Das Bemerkenswerteste an den Schönbrunner Prunkräumen ist die persönliche Anteilnahme der kaiserlichen Familie, mit der sie die Inneneinrichtung ergänzte und gestaltete. Die künstlerische Ausschmückung dieser Räume diente nicht dazu, die altbekannten Herrschertugenden allegorisch darzustellen, die Geschichte der Dynastie zu glorifizieren oder auch nur einfach Macht und Reichtum zu demonstrieren, sondern sie führt das Familienideal, um nicht zu sagen die Familienidylle der „allgemeinen und ersten Mutter" des Reiches vor.

Das Porzellanzimmer hat seinen Namen vom blau-weiß bemalten, holzgeschnitzten Rahmenwerk an den Wänden des Raumes, das Porzellan imitiert. Eine besondere Note erhält diese Dekoration durch die gekreuzten ostasiatischen Schirme, die mit Maschen verknüpft sind. In die Wandfelder sind 213 rechteckige Bilder in glatten Rahmen eingelassen, blaue Tuschzeichnungen auf Papier, Kopien nach zeitgenössischen französischen Vorlagen. Kaiser Franz I. und zwei seiner Töchter haben die Bilder gemalt, die gesamte Ausstattung hat Isabella von Parma, die Gemahlin Josephs II., entworfen. In vier Medaillons sind drei der genannten „kaiserlichen Künstler" porträtiert; zu ihnen gesellt sich als vierter Herzog Albert zu Sachsen-Teschen, der Gemahl der Erzherzogin Maria Christine. Ein sechsarmiger Luster und eine Uhr aus Meißner Porzellan in einer der fensterseitigen Ecken ergänzen die Ausstattung des Raumes.

62   Details aus den Landschaftsbildern von Joseph Rosa in den „Rosa-Zimmern" und von den Fauteuils im Gobelinsalon.

63   Das Große Rosa-Zimmer mit einem Porträt der Kaiserin Maria Theresia.

Zu den typischen Repräsentationsräumen des Schlosses zählen die drei Zimmer an der Gartenfront, zwischen Spiegelzimmer und rundem chinesischem Kabinett gelegen, in denen Gemälde angebracht sind, die Joseph Rosa geschaffen hat. Der Künstler entstammt der deutsch-niederländischen Malerfamilie Roos und war in Dresden tätig, ehe er 1772 von Joseph II. als Direktor der kaiserlichen Gemäldegalerie nach Wien berufen wurde. Die Serie von alpinen Landschaften mit Bauern, Hirten und Herden entstand schon in den Jahren 1760 bis 1765, noch während seiner Zeit als königlich polnischer Kammermaler. Er weilte also etwa zur gleichen Zeit in Wien wie Bellotto, der ja auch aus Dresden kam. Aus den Landschaften Rosas spricht jene frühromantische Begeisterung für die Natur, aber auch für die Geschichte, wenn auf einem der Gemälde im großen Zimmer die Ruine Habsburg im Aargau dargestellt wird. Im selben Raum hängt heute auch ein Porträt der Kaiserin Maria Theresia, die die merkwürdige Idee hatte, wilde schweizerische Berge in Rokokorahmen zu bannen.

wealth. On the contrary, it serves to illustrate the ideal of the family – not to mention the family idyll of the "first and universal mother" of the empire.

The Porcelain Room owes its name to the blue-and-white painted wood-carved ornaments adorning the walls, intended to imitate china. The decoration receives its special flair from the crossed East Asian umbrellas joined together by carved bows. The wall panels are decorated with 216 rectangular drawings in simple frames; the Indian ink drawings are copies of contemporary French paintings. Emperor Francis I and two of this daughters rendered the drawings, with the interior design being the work of Isabella of Parma, Joseph II's wife. Of the four portrait medaillons, three represent the "imperial artists"; the fourth shows Duke Albert zu Sachsen-Teschen, the husband of Archduchess Maria Christine. A six-armed chandelier and a clock of Meissen china in one of the corners by the windows complete the furnishings of the room.

62   Details from the landscape paintings by Joseph Rosa in the Rosa Rooms and from the arm-chairs in the "Gobelin" Room.

63   The Large Rosa Room with a portrait of Empress Maria Theresa.

The three typical state rooms on the side of palace facing the garden, between the Round Chinese Room and the Room of Mirrors, contain paintings by Joseph Rosa. The artist, the offspring of a German-Dutch family of painters bearing the name Roos, was active in Dresden before being called to Vienna by Joseph II, in 1772, to be Director of the Imperial Art Gallery. The series of depictions of Alpine landscapes with peasants and herdsmen originated in the years between 1760 and 1765, while he was still Painter to the King of Poland. The time of his residence in Vienna coincided with that of Bellotto who had also come from Dresden. Rosa's landscapes betray, in addition to the enthusiasm for nature typical of early Romanticism, and appreciation of history – as the depiction of the Hapsburg ruin in Aargau found in the large "Rosa" room conveys. In the same room hangs a portrait of Maria Theresa, who had the rather curious idea of combining the rugged mountains of Switzerland with rococo frames.

64/65   Murals by Johann Bergl (Bergl Rooms). – Illustrations from a scientific work by the botanist Nicolaus Joseph von Jacquin.

In 1891 paintings came to light from behind the gray wall-hangings of a few rooms of the east wing ground floor. They were the murals by Johann Bergl, completed partly with the assistance of Martin Steinrucker, which he had created in the years 1769 to 1777.

To enter these rooms is to enter into a strange and exotic realm. The walls and ceilings convey the illusion of a wide expanse inhabited by strange birds and animals. Here, too, the observer does not encounter untouched nature. Instead, we peer over balustrades and rococo vases, and through arcades and arches, into the parks of splendid villas and temples. The foreground is overgrown with proliferating plants and multi-shaped fruits. Nevertheless it must not be overlooked that the exact depictions of flora and fauna must have been

laine. On a encastré dans les panneaux du mur 213 tableaux rectangulaires dans des cadres lisses: des dessins à l'encre de Chine bleue sur papier, des copies de modèles français de l'époque. L'empereur François Ier et deux de ses filles ont peint les tableaux; c'est la femme de Joseph II, Isabelle de Parme qui a conçu toute la décoration. Trois des „artistes impériaux" mentionnés ci-dessus sont portraités dans les quatre médaillons de la pièce; le quatrième représente le duc Albert de Saxe-Teschen, l'époux de l'archiduchesse Marie-Christine. Un lustre à six branches et une pendule en porcelaine de Meissen complètent le décor de la pièce.

62   Détails des paysages de Joseph Rosa dans les „salons de Rosa" et des fauteuils du salon des tapisseries.

63   Le grand salon de Rosa avec un portrait de l'impératrice Marie-Thérèse.

Les trois salons situés sur le jardin entre la salle des Glaces et le cabinet chinois rond comptent au nombre des pièces de représentation typiques du château; on a encastré dans leurs murs des tableaux de Joseph Rosa. L'artiste descend d'une famille de peintres germano-hollandaise, la famille Roos et travailla à Dresde avant que Joseph II ne l'appelât à Vienne en 1772 pour devenir le directeur de la galerie impériale de peinture. La série de paysages alpestres fut peinte entre 1760 et 1765 encore au moment où il était peintre du roi de Pologne. Il séjourna à Vienne à peu près à la même époque que Bellotto qui venait aussi de Dresde. Les paysages de Rosa expriment l'enthousiasme du début du romantisme pour la nature mais aussi pour l'histoire: sur l'un des tableaux du Grand Salon, il a représenté les ruines du château de Habsbourg dans le canton d'Argovie. Dans cette pièce, il y a aujourd'hui également un portrait de l'impératrice Marie-Thérèse qui eut la curieuse idée de faire encastrer ces sauvages montagnes suisses dans un cadre rococo.

64/65   Peintures murales dans les salles de Bergl. – Illustrations provenant d'un ouvrage scientifique du botaniste Nicolaus Joseph von Jacquin.

En 1891, on découvrit sous les tentures grises de quelques pièces du rez-de-chaussée de l'aile est du château les peintures murales de Johann Bergl qu'il avait créées dans les années 1769 à 1777, en partie avec le peintre Martin Steinrucker. C'est un monde d'un exotisme étrange qui nous environne ici. Les murs et les plafonds sont recouverts d'une peinture de paysages qui donne l'illusion d'un monde lointain animé par des oiseaux et des animaux étranges. Le premier plan représente un foisonnement exubérant de plantes et de fruits de toutes sortes. On ne peut ne pas remarquer que Bergl a fait des reproductions si exactes des animaux et des plantes qu'elles doivent être fondées sur des études d'après nature qu'il aurait pu faire sans difficulté dans les serres de Schönbrunn. Sans doute, il aura aussi maintes fois fait appel aux botanistes lorsqu'il a fait entrer le monde des tropiques dans les pièces fraîches du rez-de-chaussée. Elles ont, paraît-il, servi à Marie-Thérèse de „pièces pour l'été" lorsque celles de l'étage d'apparat devenaient suffocantes.

61   La Stanza delle porcellane con il medaglione dell'Arciduchessa Maria Cristina.

Ciò che colpisce a Schönbrunn, soprattutto nelle stanze più lussuose, è il contributo personale della famiglia imperiale all'arredamento degli interni. Nella decorazione artistica di questi locali i temi ricorrenti non sono solo la rappresentazione allegorica delle note virtù della famiglia, della sua potenza e ricchezza, o la glorificazione della storia della dinastia; spesso invece si sottolinea l'ideale della famiglia, si potrebbe dire l'idillio „della comune, prime madre".
La stanza della porcellana deve il suo nome alle cornici di legno intagliato delle pareti, dipinte in bianco e azzurro, che imitano la porcellana. Una nota particolare è data dagli ombrellini incrociati (motivo proveniente dall'Asia Orientale) legati con dei fiocchi. Nelle pareti sono inseriti, in cornici lisce, duecentotredici quadri, di forma rettangolare: si tratta di disegni a china blu, su carta, copie di modelli francesi dell'epoca. Sono opera dell'Imperatore Francesco I e di due figlie. Isabella di Parma, moglie di Giuseppe II, aveva fatto il progetto della stanza. In quattro medaglioni è inserito il ritratto dei tre „artisti imperiali"; essi sono accompagnati dal duca Alberto di Sassonia-Teschen, marito dell'Arciduchessa Maria Cristina. Un lampadario a sei braccia e un orologio in porcellana di Meissen, collocato in un angolo, completano l'arredamento del locale.

62   Quadri paesaggistici di Joseph Rosa nelle Stanze di Rosa e le poltrone nel Salone degli arazzi. (Particolari).

63   La grande Stanza di Rosa con un ritratto dell'Imperatrice Maria Teresa.

Tra la stanza degli specchi e la piccola stanza cinese rotonda, vi sono, verso il giardino, tre stanze, tipici ambienti di rappresentanza, dove si trovano dei dipinti di Giuseppe Rosa. L'artista proveniva dalla famiglia di pittori tedesco-fiamminga Roos; lavorò a Dresda, prima di essere chiamato a Vienna da Giuseppe II nel 1772, dove diresse la galleria imperiale. La serie dei paesaggi alpini con contadini, pastori e greggi, risalgono agli anni 1760-1765, quando l'artista era al servizio del Re di Polonia. Fu a Vienna contemporaneamente a Bellotto, che aveva pure operato a Dresda. I paesaggi di Rosa sono pervasi da quell'entusiasmo preromantico per la natura e per la storia; e questo fatto è particolarmente evidente in uno dei dipinti nella grande stanza che rappresenta i resti della fortezza di Habsburg nell'Aargau. Qui si trova ancora oggi un ritratto di Maria Teresa che ebbe la strana idea di rinchiudere in cornici rococò le selvagge montagne svizzere.

64/65   Affreschi delle Stanze di Bergl. – Illustrazioni da un'opera scientifica del botanico Nicolaus Joseph von Jacquin.

Nel 1891, al di sotto di una copertura in tessuto, in alcuni locali nella parte est del pianterreno del castello, si possono ammirare degli affreschi di Giovanni Bergl, ai quali l'artista aveva lavorato negli anni 1769-1777 in parte da solo, in parte col collega Martino Steinrucker. È questo un mondo strano, bizzarro; le pareti e il soffitto sono decorati con dei paesaggi che danno l'idea dell'ampiezza, ravvivati da uccelli e da animali esotici. Non è questa certo una natura vergine: attraverso archi e passaggi di un giardino (che ricorda da vicino i

64/65 *Wandmalereien in den Bergl-Zimmern. –*
Illustrationen aus einem wissenschaftlichen Werk des
Botanikers Nicolaus Joseph von Jacquin.

Im Jahre 1891 entdeckte man unter der grauen Wandbespannung – man nannte sie damals Spalierung – einiger Räume im östlichen Erdgeschoßtrakt des Schlosses die Wandmalerei Johann Bergls wieder, die er 1769–1777, teilweise gemeinsam mit Martin Steinrucker, geschaffen hatte.

Es ist eine eigenartig exotische Welt, die einen hier umfängt. Wände und Decken sind von einer Landschaftsmalerei bedeckt, die die Illusion einer weiten, von fremdartigen Vögeln und Tieren belebten Welt vermittelt. Auch hier tritt uns nicht die unberührte Natur entgegen, denn durch Laubengänge und Bögen einer Gartenarchitektur, wie sie uns auch im Kammergarten begegnet, blicken wir über Balustraden und an Rokokovasen vorbei in die Gärten prächtiger Villen und Tempel. Der Vordergrund ist mit üppig wuchernden Pflanzen und vielgestaltigen Früchten ausgefüllt. Es ist nicht zu übersehen, daß Bergl exakte Darstellungen von Tieren und Pflanzen gegeben hat, die auf Naturstudien beruhen müssen, die er ohne Schwierigkeiten in den Schönbrunner Glashäusern gemacht haben könnte. Auch bei den Botanikern mag er sich so manchen Rat geholt haben, als er die Welt der Tropen in die kühlen Räume des Erdgeschoßes hereinholen wollte. Maria Theresia sollen sie als „Sommerzimmer" gedient haben, wenn es ihr in der Nobeletage zu schwül wurde.

66 *Maria Ludovica von Toskana mit ihren Kindern.*
Gemälde von Anton von Maron, um 1770. –
Peter Leopold von Toskana und sein Bruder, Joseph II.
Gemälde von Pompeo Batoni, 1769. (Vieux-Laque-Zimmer.)

Diese beiden Familienbilder im Vieux-Laque-Zimmer hängen einander gegenüber, das lebensvolle Bild Franz Stephans gleichsam flankierend (Seite 56/57). Dieser drei Gemälde wegen, entstanden zwischen 1769 und 1773, liebte Maria Theresia das Zimmer besonders. Sind doch ihr verstorbener Gatte, der „einzige Geliebte", die beiden hochbegabten Söhne, denen die Zukunft anvertraut war, und – auf dem Bild von Anton Maron – der erste Enkel auf dem Schoß der Schwiegertochter dargestellt! Um ihr Glück über die Geburt des kleinen Franz (1768) den Wienern mitzuteilen, eilte sie ins Hofburgtheater, in dem sie sich seit dem Tod ihres Gatten nicht mehr gezeigt hatte. Die Darstellung der beiden Brüder in Rom erregte schon damals Bewunderung wegen der Natürlichkeit, mit der ihr Zusammentreffen wiedergegeben ist. Bedauerlicherweise ging das Originalbild nach dem Ende des Zweiten Weltkrieges verloren und wurde durch eine Kopie ersetzt. Hier abgebildet ist die erste Fassung von 1769, die in der Gemäldegalerie des Kunsthistorischen Museums hängt.

Joseph weilte während einer Inspektionsreise durch die italienischen Provinzen in Rom – wie es sich für ihn gehörte: inkognito! Und doch wußte man um die historische Stunde. Seit Karl V. war wieder ein Kaiser in der Ewigen Stadt. Das Gemälde aber sagt noch mehr: Joseph, der Ältere, ist scharfsinnig und ehrgeizig, spottlustig, aber selbst leicht verletzbar. Er wird zum Idol der jungen Deutschen, auf ihn hoffen die Intellektuellen einer neuen Zeit; Herder, Lessing, Goethe und Schiller schreiben begeistert über ihn. Allzufrüh endet er, ohne die Früchte seiner unmenschlichen Anstrengungen als Staatsoberhaupt zu ernten.

Leopold hingegen ist ausgeglichen und ausgleichend, intuitiv,

modeled after detailed sketches that Bergl could easily have drawn in the various hothouses of Schönbrunn. It is also likely that the expertise of a botanist helped him suffuse the cold rooms of the ground floor with the warmth of the tropics. The rooms are said to have been used by Maria Theresa as "summer quarters" when it became too humid on the upper floors.

66 *Maria Ludovica of Tuscany and her children.*
Painting by Anton von Maron, c. 1770. –
Peter Leopold of Tuscany and his brother, Joseph II.
Painting by Pompeo Batoni, 1769. ("Vieux-Laque" Room.)

These two family portraits in the Vieux-Laque Room hang opposite one another and flank the life-like painting of her husband (pages 56/57). Maria Theresa was partial to the room precisely on account of these three paintings completed between 1769 and 1773. They do depict, after all, her deceased husband and "only beloved", the two highly talented sons to whom the future would be entrusted, and – in Anton Maron's portrait – the first grandson on the lap of her daughter-in-law! In order to announce her happiness at the birth of little Francis (1768) to all of Vienna she hurried to the "Hofburg" Theatre, which she had not entered since the death of her husband.

The painting of the two brothers in Rome was admired even at the time for its naturalistic portrayal of the brothers' reunion. Unfortunately, the original was lost after the end of the Second World War and had to be replaced by a copy. Pictured here is the original of 1769 which is displayed in the picture gallery of the Kunsthistorisches Museum.

On an inspection journey through the Italian provinces, Joseph traveled to Rome in the manner he had deemed proper: incognito! Nevertheless one was aware of the historic hour: since Charles V, no Emperor had set foot in Rome. But the painting conveys even more: Joseph, the older of the two, is ingenious and ambitious, outwardly sarcastic but inwardly vulnerable. He became the idol of the young Germans and the hope of the intellectuals of a dawning age: Herder, Lessing, Goethe, and Schiller all wrote glowingly of him. But he died all too soon without having been able to reap the fruits of his superhuman efforts as sovereign.

Leopold, on the other hand, is well-balanced and conciliatory, intuitive, gentle and warmly human. He, too, recognizes early the deficiencies of the Vienna Court, but also those of his brother, whose successor he would eventually become. His advice on the rearing of children also echoes the feelings of his brother, Joseph: "Sovereigns must, above all, be convinced of the equality of people . . ."

Joseph's ideas and far-reaching reforms came too soon for some but continued to transform the empire long after his death. The painting succeeds in capturing the unquestionable integrity of his intentions. Georg Forster wrote of him: "From the torch of his spirit a spark has fallen that will never be extinguished."

66   *Maria Ludovica de Toscane avec ses enfants. Peinture de Anton von Maron, vers 1770. –*
Pierre Léopold de Toscane et son frére, Joseph II.
Peinture de Pompeo Batoni, 1769. (Salon Vieux-Laque.)

Ces deux portraits de famille sont suspendus l'un en face de l'autre, dans le salon Vieux-Laque, de chaque côté du portrait si vivant de François de Lorraine (pages 56/57). Marie-Thérèse aimait particulièrement cette pièce à cause de ces trois tableaux, peints entre 1769 et 1773. Ne représentent-ils pas son défunt époux, l'„unique bien-aimé", les deux fils si doués à qui l'avenir était confié et, – sur le tableau d'Anton Maron – le premier petit-fils sur les genoux de sa bru! Pour faire part de son bonheur aux Viennois, lors de la naissance du petit Franz (1768), elle se rendit en hâte au Hofburgtheater ou elle ne s'était plus montrée depuis la mort de son epoux bien-aimé.

La représentation des deux frères à Rome avait déjà fait naître l'admiration à cette époque à cause du naturel avec lequel leur rencontre avait été peinte. Malheureusement, le tableau original disparut à la fin de la deuxième guerre mondiale et fut remplacé par une copie. Sur l'image, vous voyez la première version de 1769, qui est suspendue dans la galerie des portraits du musée des Beaux-Arts. Pendant un voyage d'inspection à travers les provinces italiennes, Joseph séjourna à Rome – incognito – comme il se doit. Et cependant, on connaissait l'heure historique. Depuis Charles-Quint, il n'y avait pas eu d'empereur dans la Ville Eternelle. Mais le tableau nous en dit encore bien davantage:

Joseph, l'aîné, est subtil et ambitieux, railleur mais facilement blessé lui-même. Il devient l'idole des jeunes Allemands; les intellectuels d'une nouvelle époque mettent leurs espérances en lui; Herder, Lessing, Goethe et Schiller écrivent avec enthousiasme à son sujet. Il meurt bien trop tôt sans pouvoir récolter les fruits de ses efforts humains en tant que chef d'Etat.

Par contre, Leopold est pondéré et équilibré, intuitif, prudent et très humain. Il reconnait tôt les fautes de la cour de Vienne mais aussi celles de son frère dont il devait devenir le successeur en tant qu'empereur. On possède de lui une instruction pour l'education des enfants qui réfléchit aussi les sentiments de Joseph: „Les princes doivent être surtout persuadés de l'égalité des hommes ..."

Les idées de Joseph et ses réformes à grande portée vinrent trop tôt pour certains et furent la cause bien après sa mort d'une réorganisation du royaume. On ne peut douter de sa sincérité ni de sa bonne volonté; c'est aussi ce que nous montre ce tableau. Georg Forster dit: „Du flambeau de son esprit est tombée une étincelle qui ne s'éteindra plus jamais".

giardini imperiali!) godiamo di una splendida vista sui parchi che circondano meravigliose ville e templi. Su balaustrate poggiano vasi rococò, mentre in primo piano ci sono richissime piante e frutta diversa. Va osservato che Bergl è stato molto preciso nel dipingere animali e piante. Senza dubbio egli aveva preparato degli studi nelle ricche serre di Schönbrunn. Sicuramente gli sono stati d'aiuto anche i consigli fornitigli da alcuni botanici, soprattutto per quanto riguarda la raffigurazione dell'ambiente vegetale dei tropici. Maria Teresa utilizzava queste stanze come „stanze per l'estate", quando al piano nobile faceva troppo caldo.

66   *Maria Ludovica di Toscana con i figli. Dipinto di Anton von Maron, intorno al 1770. –*
Pietro Leopoldo di Toscana e suo fratello, Giuseppe II.
Dipinto di Pompeo Batoni, 1769. (Stanza vieux-laque.)

Questi du dipinti, che si trovano nella Stanza vieux-laque, sono posti l'uno di fronte all'altro e sono a lato del delizioso quadro che ritrae Francesco Stefano (pag. 56/57). Maria Teresa amava particolarmente questa stanza per via dei tre quadri, dipinti tra il 1769 e il 1773. Essi ritraggono rispettivamente il marito, deceduto, l'„unico uomo amato", i due figli più dotati, che avevano nelle proprie mani il futuro del regno, e, nel quadro di Antonio Maron, il primo nipotino che era in braccio alla propria madre. Per dimostrare ai viennesi la sua felicità per la nascita del piccolo Francesco (1768), Maria Teresa si recò immediatamente al Burgtheater, nel quale non aveva più messo piede dalla morte del marito.

La raffigurazione dei due fratelli a Roma aveva già suscitato l'ammirazione di tutti per la naturalezza che vi si riscontrava. Purtroppo, alla fine della seconda guerra mondiale, il quadro originale andò perduto; è stato sostituito da una copia che si rifà al primo modello del 1769, esposta nella Pinacoteca del Museo di storia dell'arte.

Durante un viaggio di ispezione attraverso le Province italiane, Giuseppe sostò a Roma, in incognito, come era sua abitudine. Tuttavia la cosa si venne a sapere. Era un momento storico, in quanto, dall'epoca di Carlo V, nessun imperatore aveva più messo piede nella Città Eterna. Ma il dipinto ha un significato ancora più profondo. Giuseppe, il figlio maggiore di Maria Teresa, è un uomo acuto ed ambizioso, beffardo, ma suscettibile. Diventa l'idolo dei giovani tedeschi; gli intellettuali vedono giungere tempi nuovi. Herder, Lessing, Goethe e Schiller hanno per lui parole di grande ammirazione. Troppo presto muore senza poter cogliere i frutti delle sue sovrumane fatiche quale capo di stato.

Leopoldo è invece equilibrato, accomodante, intuitivo, accorto, umanissimo. Ben presto riconosce gli errori commessi dalla corte di Vienna, anche quelli del proprio fratello, al quale succederà, diventando lui imperatore.

Rispecchia l'idea del fratello Giuseppe quella riguardante l'educazione dei giovani: „I principi, prima degli altri, debbono essere convinti che tutti gli uomini sono uguali ..."

Le idee di Giuseppe e le sue innovatrici riforme erano, per alcuni, premature; però, anche dopo la sua morte diedero origine a una positiva trasformazione del regno. E' indiscutibile l'onestà dei suoi intenti. Questo lo mostra anche il dipinto. Giorgio Forster dice: „Dalla fiaccola del suo spirito è caduta una scintilla che non si spegnerà mai".

behutsam und voller Menschlichkeit. Auch er erkennt frühzeitig die Fehler des Wiener Hofes, aber auch die seines Bruders, dessen Nachfolger als Kaiser er werden sollte. Von ihm ist eine Anweisung zur Erziehung der Kinder erhalten, die auch Josephs Gefühle widerspiegelt: „Fürsten müssen vor allen anderen von der Gleichheit der Menschen überzeugt sein . . ."
Josephs Ideen und weitreichende Reformen kamen für manche zu früh und bewirkten eine weit über seinen Tod hinausreichende Umgestaltung des Reichs. Die Lauterkeit seines Wollens ist unbezweifelbar, und auch das zeigt uns dieses Bild. „Aus der Fackel seines Geistes ist ein Funke gefallen, der nie wieder erlischt", sagt Georg Forster.

67   Die Gartenseite des Schlosses. Gemälde von Bernardo Bellotto, um 1760. – Details aus den Wandmalereien der Bergl-Zimmer.

Bernardo Bellottos Ansichten des Schönbrunner Schlosses sind unschätzbare Zeugnisse für dessen Aussehen und für seine Lage außerhalb Wiens (Seiten 8/9). Auf der Vedute von der Gartenseite erkennen wir weit hinten den Turm der Stephanskirche und die Kuppel der Karlskirche. In Schönbrunn war die kaiserliche Familie wirklich „am Land". Die Wiedergabe der gärtnerischen Gestaltung des Parketts ist besonders aufschlußreich. Wir sehen es in dem Zustand, der durch die Änderungen herbeigeführt worden war, die Maria Theresia offenbar schon in den fünfziger Jahren veranlaßt hatte.
Anstelle der Ornamente aus Steinen und niederen Gebüschen, die wie Stickereimuster aussahen und zur Bezeichnung „Broderieparterres" Anlaß gaben, sehen wir größere Rasenflächen, die von Kreisen und Spiralen unterbrochen sind, die bis zum Rand verlaufen, sodaß die Rasenkonturen unterbrochen werden. Die Mitte dieser Rasenflächen ist vertieft angelegt, was man sich heute nicht mehr recht erklären kann. Waren diese Flächen für ein Ballspiel gedacht? In der Mittelachse vor dem Schloß hatte man damals noch das Sternbassin Fischers von Erlach belassen. An den Längsseiten sind die Rasenflächen von Rosenbeeten begrenzt. Dazu parallel laufen Reihen von Orangenbäumchen in Holzkübeln („Pommerantzen Khüebeln") und schmale Rabatte mit spitzen Taxusbäumchen. Die Skulpturen, die heute das Parkett säumen, fehlen hingegen noch.
Das Bild befindet sich im Kunsthistorischen Museum.

68/69   Die Nymphe Egeria am „Schönen Brunnen" und der Najadenbrunnen im östlichen Rundbassin von Wilhelm Beyer.

Dem Kaiser Matthias (1612–1619) wird die Entdeckung jener Quelle zugeschrieben, die dem Schloß Schönbrunn den Namen gab. Jedenfalls wurde ein heute noch vorhandener Quellstein mit seinen Initialen errichtet und die Quelle gefaßt. Eine weibliche Figur, aus deren Brüsten Wasser floß, wurde 1683 zerstört. Erst unter Maria Theresia erbaute man über der Quelle ein grottenartiges Brunnenhäuschen und beauftragte den Bildhauer Wilhelm Beyer, eine neue Statue zu schaffen. Er entschloß sich zur Darstellung der altrömischen Nymphe Egeria, die der Sage nach den zweiten König Roms, Numa Pompilius, einen Friedensfürsten, beraten haben soll. Ihr war an der Via Appia eine Grotte geweiht, die noch heute bosco sacro – heiliger Wald – genannt wird.

67   The garden façade of Schönbrunn Palace. Painting by Bernardo Bellotto, c. 1760. – Details from the murals in the Bergl Rooms.

Bernardo Bellotto's vedutas (pages 8/9) are invaluable testimony to the appearance of the palace and its location outside of Vienna. In the view of the garden facade, both the spire of St. Stephen's Cathedral and the dome of St. Charles' can be seen in the distance. At Schönbrunn the imperial family was truly "in the country-side". The depiction of the layout of the parterre is especially instructive. The painting shows the alterations that Maria Theresa had obviously already carried out in the fifties.
In place of stone and shrubbery ornaments that looked like embroidery and gave rise to the term "Broderieparterres", we find large lawns partitioned by circular and spiral paths that extend to the edges of the lawn and interrupt its contours. The centres of these lawn areas are at a lower level than the rest, a fact which is difficult to explain today. Where these areas intended for some sort of ballgame? In the middle avenue, in front of the palace, Fischer von Erlach's star-shaped basin still had been left as it was. Along the longitudinal edges the lawns are bordered by rosebeds; parallel to them were placed rows of orange trees in wooden pots, and narrow borders of pointed yew trees. The statuary bordering the parterre today was still absent then.

68/69   The nymph Egeria at the "Beautiful Spring" and the Fountain of the Naiad in the eastern round basin, both by Wilhelm Beyer.

The discovery of the spring from which Schönbrunn derives its name is attributed to Emperor Matthias (1612-1619). In any event, a well-head with his initials, which is still today, was erected and the spring channeled into a small basin. A figurine of a woman whose breasts dispensed water was destroyed in 1683. Not until Maria Theresa's reign was the small grotto-like well-house built and the sculptor Wilhelm Beyer commissioned to create a new statue. He decided on a representation of the mythological Roman nymph Egeria, who, according to legend, is said to have advised the second and peace-loving king of Rome, Numa Pompilius. On the Via Appia a grotto was dedicated to her that is still called bosco sacro (sacred grove).

70   The "French" park with statuary and with the "Roman Ruin" by Ferdinand von Hohenberg, c. 1775.

The phenomenon of intertwining nature and architecture has been mentioned repeatedly in connection with the Baroque. At Schönbrunn a true harmony of style was never achieved because work was prolonged over a period of years. The sculpture ornamentation and the most important landscaping were not completed, after many modifications, until the seventies – thereby introducing neo-classical elements into a park that had already suffered the transitions from the Baroque to the Rococo. The placement of the individual statues was also subject to repeated alterations. The thematic design had been proposed by State Chancellor Prince Anton Wenzel Kaunitz; he intended a mythological and historical illustration of nature, incorporating political allusions and pedagogical aspects.

67 Le château côté jardin. Tableau de Bernardo Bellotto, vers 1760. –
Détails des peintures murales des salles de Bergl.

Les vues du château de Schönbrunn de Bernardo Bellotto (pages 8/9) sont des témoignages inestimables de son aspect et de sa situation en dehors de Vienne. Sur la perspective du côté jardin, on reconnait au loin la tour de Saint-Etienne et la coupole de l'eglise Saint-Charles. A Schönbrunn, la famille impériale était vraiment „à la campagne". Nous voyons le jardin tel qu'il était après les remaniements que Marie-Thérèse avait déjà probablement fait effectuer dans les années cinquante. A la place des ornements de pierre et des buissons bas qui ressemblaient à des motifs de broderie et qui furent à l'origine du nom „parterres de broderie", nous voyons de plus grandes pelouses, entrecoupées par des cercles et des spirales qui continuent jusqu'aux bords de sorte que les contours sont discontinus. Le milieu de ces pelouses montre une dépression; pour quelle raison ont-elles été aménagées ainsi? C'est difficile à expliquer aujourd'hui. Avait-on prévu d'y jouer un jeu de balle? A cette époque, on avait encore laissé le bassin de l'Etoile de Fischer von Erlach dans l'axe médian devant le château. Dans la longueur, les pelouses sont délimités par des plates-bandes de rosiers. Des rangées d'orangers dans des caisses de bois ainsi que d'étroites bordures de petits ifs pointus sont installées parallèlement aux plates-bandes. Par contre, les statues qui bordent aujourd'hui les parterres manquent encore. Le tableau se trouve au musée des Beaux-arts.

68/69 La nymphe Egérie à la „Belle Fontaine"
et la fontaine des naïades dans le bassin rond oriental de Wilhelm Beyer.

C'est à l'empereur Matthias (1612–1619) qu'on attribue la découverte de la source qui donna son nom au château de Schönbrunn. En tout cas, il existe encore aujourd'hui une plaque commémorative de la découverte avec ses initiales et la source fut captée. Une statue de femme des seins de laquelle l'eau s'écoulait fut détruite en 1683. Ce fut seulement sous Marie-Thérèse qu'on construisit au-dessus de la fontaine un pavillon en forme de grotte et qu'on commanda une nouvelle statue au sculpteur Wilhelm Beyer. Il décida de représenter une nymphe de l'ancienne Rome. Egérie qui, d'après la légende, fut la conseillère du deuxième roi de Rome, Numa Pompilius, un prince da la paix. On lui avait consacré une grotte sur la Via Appia qui s'appelle encore aujourd'hui bosco sacro – bois sacré.

70 Le parc „à la française" avec des sculptures et avec la „ruine romaine" de Ferdinand de Hohenberg, vers 1775.

Une unité dans le style n'a jamais été atteinte à Schönbrunn car les travaux se prolongèrent pendant plusieurs dizaine d'années. La décoration sculpturale ainsi que les œuvres les plus importantes de l'architecture paysagiste ne furent terminées que dans les années 70 et apportèrent donc ainsi des éléments essentiels du style néo-classique à un jardin qui avait déjà subi le passage du baroque au rococo. A la fin, on hésite sur l'emplacement des différentes statues. Le concept thématique est dû au chancelier d'Etat, le prince Anton Wenzel Kaunitz. C'était dans son intention d'illustrer la nature de manière mythologique et historique en y incluant des allusions politiques; cette illustration devait également être instrucitve.

67 Facciata del castello vista dal giardino. Dipinto di Bernardo Bellotto, intorno al 1760. –
Affreschi nelle Stanze di Bergl. (Particolari).

Le vedute di Schönbrunn (pag. 8, 9), opera di Bernardo Bellotto, sono inestimabili testimonianze che ci mostrano quale era l'aspetto e la posizione del Castello rispetto a Vienna.
Nella veduta della parte verso il giardino sono riconoscibili, sullo sfondo, il campanile di S. Stefano e la cupola di S. Carlo. A Schönbrunn la famiglia era realmente „in campagna". Il dipinto rende perfettamente l'idea del tipo di giardino che vi era all'epoca e delle modifiche che Maria Teresa vi aveva fatto apportare evidentemente già intorno al 1750.
Al posto di abbellimenti in pietra e bassi cespugli, tali da far assomigliare questo giardino ad un ricamo (donde il nome giardino à broderie), vediamo delle grandi aiole, interrotte da cerchi e da spirali, che giungono fino al limite estremo del giardino stesso. Il centro di queste aiole era incavato, oggi ben difficilmente spiegabile. Forse queste superfici erano pensate per dei giochi. Nella parte centrale davanti al castello si trovava ancora la fontana, a forma di stella, di Fischer von Erlach. Nelle parti longitudinali le aiole sono delimitate da cespugli di rose. Parallelamente a questi corrono delle file di aranci piantati in mastelli di legno e strette aiole con alberi di tasso. Non erano ancora presenti le sculture che oggi delimitano il giardino. Il quadro si trova nel Museo di storia dell'arte.

68/69 La ninfa Egeria seduta alla sorgente d'acqua „Bella Fontana" e la fontana delle Najadi nella piscina rotonda di Wilhelm Beyer.

Si deve all'Imperatore Matteo (1612–1619) la scoperta di quella sorgente d'acqua che diede il nome al castello di Schönbrunn. Ancor oggi si può ammirare la lapide commemorativa, con le iniziali dello Imperatore, là dove la sorgente fu incanalata. Nel 1683 fu distrutta una statua dal cui seno sgorgava l'acqua della sorgente. Maria Teresa fece costruire, al di sopra della sorgente, un riparo a forma di grotta e affidò allo scultore Guglielmo Beyer il compito di scolpire una nuova statua. Costui raffigurò la ninfa Egeria che appartiene alla tradizione antico-romana. Secondo la leggenda, questa era la consigliera del pacifico Re di Roma, Numa Pompilio. Al lei è dedicata ancor oggi, sulla Via Appia, uno grotta chiamata appunto „bosco sacro".

70 Il parco „francese" con sculture e con le „Rovine Romane" di Ferdinand von Hohenberg, intorno al 1775.

Nel giardino barocco, come si ebbe già a dire, natura ed architettura sono profondamente compenetrate. A Schönbrunn non si riscontra un'unità stilistica in quanto i lavori si sono protratti per decenni. Le sculture, così come le opere architettoniche del giardino, subirono molte trasformazioni e solo verso il 1770 questo acquista la sua struttura definitiva. Furono inseriti elementi classicheggianti in un ambiente che rappresenta già chiaramente il passaggio dal Barocco al Rococò. La collocazione delle singole statue fu un'operazione che richiese riflessione; si ha ragione di credere che furono fatti diversi tentativi prima di giungere alla sistemazione definitiva.
Il Cancelliere di stato, Principe Antonio Wenzel Kaunitz, aveva stabilito che cosa dovesse rappresentare il giardino di Schönbrunn:

70 Der „französische" Park mit Skulpturen und mit der „Römischen Ruine" von Ferdinand von Hohenberg, um 1775.

Wiederholt wurde auf das Phänomen der Durchdringung von Natur und Architektur im barocken Lustgarten hingewiesen. In Schönbrunn ist niemals ein stilistisch einheitlicher Zustand erreicht worden, da sich die Arbeiten jahrzehntelang hinzogen. Der Skulpturenschmuck sowie die wichtigsten Werke der Parkarchitektur wurden erst nach mehrmaliger Planänderung in den siebziger Jahren fertiggestellt, brachten also wesentliche Elemente des Klassizismus in einen Garten, der seinerseits bereits die Wandlung vom Barock zum Rokoko erduldet hatte. Über die Aufstellung der einzelnen Skulpturen war man sich schließlich gar nicht mehr sicher, sondern änderte diese mehrmals. Das thematische Konzept hatte Staatskanzler Fürst Anton Wenzel Kaunitz entworfen. Er beabsichtigte eine mythologisch-historische Illustration der Natur, die sowohl politische Anspielungen enthielt als auch belehrend wirken sollte.

Im Jahre 1765 übernahm Ferdinand von Hohenberg die baukünstlerische Leitung der Arbeiten; um 1772 begann der Bildhauer Johann Chr. Wilhelm Beyer, der 1769 aus Gotha nach Wien gekommen war, die Skulpturen zu entwerfen und sie mit seinen Mitarbeitern auszuführen. Mehr als ein Dutzend Meister unterschiedlicher Begabung arbeiteten an den marmornen Bildwerken der Götter und Helden der Antike, die rundum im Garten aufgestellt werden sollten. An den Kreuzungspunkten der beiden diagonalen Alleen mit der mittleren, der sogenannten Linden-Allee, wurden zwei große Bassins angelegt. Das Sternbassin wurde vom Parkett, wo es vor der Freitreppe des Schlosses gewesen war – wie man auf Bellottos Gemälde sehen kann (Seite 67) – in die Tiergartenallee übertragen.

Zwischen 1775 und 1780 wurden schließlich die drei mächtigsten Werke der Gartenarchitektur nach Hohenbergs Plänen errichtet, die Gloriette (Seiten 76, 77, 96, 105), die Römische Ruine (Seiten 70, 79) und der Neptunbrunnen (Seiten 74, 84, 95). Mit diesen Bauwerken hat Hohenberg seinen Ideenreichtum und seine Meisterschaft bei der Ausführung bewiesen. Die sogenannte Römische Ruine ist dabei in jeder Hinsicht das außergewöhnlichste Werk. Schon die Barockzeit liebte Gemälde mit Ruinenphantasien, aber erst die Romantik sollte sie tatsächlich errichten, wofür es in der Umgebung Wiens nicht an Beispielen fehlt. Die Schönbrunner Ruine nimmt zwischen beiden Epochen eine eigentümliche Stellung ein. Vor der bühnenartig geöffneten Architektur mit dem mächtigen Bogen liegt ein Bassin, das den Betrachter zur Distanz zwingt. Im Wasser steht eine Figurengruppe von Beyer, angeblich die Vereinigung der Moldau mit der Elbe darstellend, die den romantischen Zug der Anlage betont. Mit einer ähnlichen Komposition – die Vereinigung der Enns mit der Donau versinnbildlichend – hat Beyer auch die Grotte geschmückt, auf die Hohenberg einen Obelisken stellte, der von einem Adler bekrönt und von vier Schildkröten getragen ist. Falsche Hieroglyphen geben vor, die Geschichte des Hauses Habsburg zu erzählen.

71 Der Kammergarten des Kaisers Franz Joseph an der Westfront des Schlosses.

Für den französischen Park sind nicht nur die großen Achsen und Flächen – die „Parterres" – kennzeichnend, sondern – wie für jede Architektur – auch die zwischen diesen liegenden kleinen Flächen und Räume. Sie wurden besonders im Rokoko phantasievoll und

In 1765 Ferdinand von Hohenberg assumed responsibility for the execution of the scheme; in 1772 the sculptor Johann Chr. Wilhelm Beyer, who had come to Vienna from Gotha in 1769, began having his assistants carry out the designs he had conceived. More than a dozen different "masters" of varying abilities worked on the marble images of the mythological gods and heroes to be placed about the park. At the intersection of the two diagonal avenues with the middle longitudinal one, the so-called "Linden Avenue", two large ponds were placed. The star-shaped basin was transferred from the avenue in front of the open-air-flight of steps – visible in Bellotto's painting (page 67) – to the avenue leading to the zoo; the round pond was newly constructed.

Between 1775 and 1780 the three most imposing constituents of the park were completed in conformance to Hohenberg's designs: the Gloriette (pages 76, 77, 96, 105); the Roman Ruins (pages 70, 79); and the Neptune Fountain (pages 74, 84, 95). With these additions Hohenberg demonstrated his wealth of vision and mastery of execution. The so-called Roman ruins are, in every respect, the most extraordinary work. Although the Baroque exhibits a predilection for paintings of fantastic ruins, Romanticism was the first epoch to see them actually erected, and there are several examples in the vicinity of Vienna. The ruin at Schönbrunn occupies a peculiar position between the two periods. In front of the open, stage-like structure with the mighty arch stands a basin, which keeps the observer at a distance. The statuary group by Beyer in the water, said to depict the confluence of the Moldau and Elbe rivers, intensifies the romantic aspects of the layout.

Beyer adorned the grotto with a similar composition – this time symbolizing the converging rivers Enns and Danube. On top of the grotto, Hohenberg placed an obelisk surmounted by an eagle and supported by four turtles. Pseudo-hieroglyphs allegedly relate the history of the House of Hapsburg.

71 The private garden of Emperor Francis Joseph along the west façade of the palace.

The French park is distinguished not only by its large avenues and terraces – called "parterres" – but also, as is all architecture, by the spaces in between. During the period of the Rococo the garden layouts were especially imaginative and varied, featuring labyrinths or mazes, shadowy ornamental shrubbery with protected enclosures, and areas devoted to the cultivation of selected plants (rosarium). In the garden layout drawn by Boos from the year 1780 (page 7), numerous such areas can be recognized, bearing such names as "fan" or "merry-go-round". The labyrinth on the west side of the large parterre, still visible in Bellotto's painting (page 67), was unfortunately cleared in 1892 out of moral considerations.

Both private gardens, laid out according to plans by Jean Nicolas Jadot soon after 1750, were reserved for the exclusive use of the imperial family already in Maria Theresa's day. In 1770 the wrought iron pergolas now overgrown with roses were erected (page 78), as were the elegant wooden pavillions with ceiling murals by the school of Bergl. The "Bergl" rooms on the ground floor of the palace illustrate not only the aesthetic, but also the philosophical connection between nature and architecture that prevailed during the Baroque.

En 1765, Ferdinand von Hohenberg fut chargé de la direction artistique des travaux; vers 1772, le sculpteur Johann Chr. Wilhelm Beyer qui était venu de Gotha à Vienne en 1769 commença à ébaucher les sculptures et à les réaliser avec ses collaborateurs. Aux carrefours des deux allées diagonales avec l'allée médiane, dite „Allée des Tilleuls", on aménagea deux grands bassins. Le bassin de l'Etoile fut transféré du parterre où il se trouvait devant le grand perron du château – comme on peut le voir sur le tableau de Bellotto (page 67) – dans l'allée du jardin zoologique tandis que le bassin rond fut reconstruit. Finalement, entre 1775 et 1780, les trois œuvres majeures de l'architecture paysagiste furent construites d'après les plans de Hohenberg: la Gloriette (pages 76, 77, 96, 105), la ruine Romaine (pages 70, 79) et le bassin de Neptune (pages 74, 84, 95). Dans ces ouvrages, Hohenberg a prouvé sa richesse d'idées et sa maîtrise dans l'exécution. La ruine Romaine est, des trois, à tout égard, l'œuvre la plus originale. Déjà, à l'époque baroque, on appréciait les tableaux aux ruines de fantaisie, mais c'est seulement à l'époque romantique qu'on les construisit vraiment; il n'en manque pas de nombreux exemples aux alentours de Vienne. La ruine de Schönbrunn occupe entre les deux époques une place toute particulière. Devant l'édifice, ouvert comme un décor de théâtre, avec son arcade puissante, est situé un bassin qui oblige à le contempler d'une certaine distance. Dans l'eau se dresse un groupe de statues de Beyer qui accentue le caractère romantique de l'ouvrage.

Beyer a aussi, avec une composition du même genre décoré la grotte sur laquelle Hohenberg dressa un obélisque couronné d'un aigle et porté par quatre tortues. Des faux hiéroglyphes prétendent raconter l'histoire de la maison de Habsbourg.

71 Le jardin de la Cour de l'empereur François-Joseph du côté de la façade occidentale du château.

Ce ne sont pas seulement les „parterres" qui sont caractéristiques du jardin à la française mais également les petits espaces et superficies situés entre eux. Ils sont aménagés, en particulier à l'époque rococo, avec beaucoup d'imagination et de manière très variée en tant que labyrinthe, bosquets ombreux aux cabinets secrets ou en tant que domaine de culture de plantes particulières („rosarium"). Sur le plan de Schönbrunn de Boos de l'année 1780 (page 7), nous pouvons reconnaitre de nombreux petits jardins de ce genre. Le labyrinthe de Schönbrunn qui avait été aménagé du côté ouest du grand parterre, comme on peut le voir à gauche sur le tableau de Bellotto (page 67), fut malheureusement détruit pour des raisons de moralité en 1892. Les deux jardins de la Cour, qui avaient été dessinés peu après 1750 d'après les plans de Jean Nicolas Jadot, etaient comme leur nom l'indique, réservés à la famille impériale déjà à l'époque de Marie-Thérèse. Vers 1790, on construisit les pergolas de fer qui, aujourd'hui, sont envahies par les rosiers grimpants (page 78) et les gracieux pavillons de bois dont les fresques du plafond proviennent d'élèves ou de collaborateurs de Bergl; avec les salles de „Bergl" au rez-de-chaussée, il existe un rapport artistique.

doveva essere una illustrazione storico-mitologica della natura (con riferimenti politici) con un fine didattico, nel contempo.
Nel 1772 lo scultore Giovanni C. Guglielmo Beyer, che proveniva da Gotha, cominciò a progettare e ad eseguire, con i suoi collaboratori, le statue. Una dozzina e più di maestri, diversi per provenienza e capacità, cominciarono a lavorare alle statue degli dei e eroi dell'antichità che dovevano trovare posto lungo il perimetro del giardino. Nei punti di incontro dei due viali diagonali con quello mediano, il cosiddetto viale dei tigli, furono collocate due grandi fontane. Quella a forma di stella che si trovava nelle immediate vicinanze del castello, là dove finiva la grande scalinata esterna, poi abbattuta (vedi il dipinto di Bellotto a pag. 67), fu sistemata nel viale del giardino zoologico. La fontana rotonda invece fu costruita ex novo.
Secondo il progetto di Hohenberg, tra il 1775 e il 1780 furono ultimate le tre opere più imponenti del giardino: la Gloriette (pagg. 76, 77, 96, 105), le Rovine Romane (pagg. 70, 79), la fontana di Nettuno (pagg. 74, 84, 95). Queste opere sono una chiara dimostrazione della ricchezza di idee e della capacità di esecuzione di Hohenberg. La costruzione più curiosa è rappresentata dalle Rovine Romane. Già il Barocco amava i dipinti con raffigurazioni di rovine. Queste però furono costruite concretamente in epoca romantica.
E intorno a Vienna gli esempi non mancano. Le rovine di Schönbrunn occupano un posto particolare in quanto sono state eseguite a cavallo di due epoche. Davanti ad un possente arco, sistemato in un grandioso ambiente naturale, è collocata una fontana, che, per essere ammirata, ha bisogno di esser vista a distanza. Nell'acqua si trova un gruppo scultoreo di Beyer che dovrebbe rappresentare l'unione della Moldava con l'Elba. Quest'opera sottolinea ulteriormente il carattere romantico del giardino. Beyer ha sistemato nella grotta un gruppo analogo (unione dell'Enns col Danubio). Al di sopra di questo, Hohenberg vi ha posto un obelisco, sostenuto da quattro tartarughe, sulla cui sommità è posata un'aquila. Dei falsi geroglifici racconterebbero la storia della Casa Asburgica.

71 Il giardino di Corte dell'Imperatore Francesco Giuseppe sul fronte ovest del castello.

Caratteristica del parco alla francese sono non solo le grandi superfici, dette „parterres" e le relative zone di congiunzione, ma, come per qualsiasi forma architettonica, gli spazi e le piccole superfici che si trovano tra questi. Particolarmente nel Rococò i giardini furono realizzati in maniera fantasiosa e varia, per esempio, come labirinto, come boschetto ombroso con angoli nascosti oppure come zone di culture particolari („Rosarium"). Nel progetto per il giardino di Schönbrunn, opera di Boos (1780 - vedi pag. 7), vediamo molte piccole zone a giardino di questo tipo. Spesso portavano nomi come „ventaglio" o „giostra", in quanto essi rispecchiavano la loro forma. Il labirinto di Schönbrunn, nella parte ovest della grande „parterre", come possiamo vedere nel dipinto di Bellotto (pag. 67) a sinistra, non esiste più dal 1892 per ragioni di moralità. Due giardini, realizzati subito dopo il 1750 secondo i progetti di Jean Nicolas Jadot, già all'epoca di Maria Teresa, erano riservati alla famiglia imperiale. Intorno al 1770 furono costruite delle arcate in ferro, oggi ricoperte di rose rampicanti (pag. 78), e furono eretti dei graziosi padiglioni in legno, i cui soffitti furono decorati da allievi e collaboratori di Bergl. Le cosiddetta stanza di Bergl, che si trovava al pianterreno del Castello e quanto descritto precedentemente, non sono un fatto

abwechslungsreich als Labyrinth oder Irrgarten, als schattige Boskette mit versteckten Kammern oder auch als Bereich besonderer Pflanzenkulturen („Rosarium") angelegt. Auf dem Schönbrunner Plan von Boos aus dem Jahr 1780 (Seite 7) können wir zahlreiche kleine Gartenbereiche dieser Art erkennen; sie trugen oft entsprechende Namen wie „Fächer" oder „Ringelspiel". Das Schönbrunner Labyrinth, das an der Westseite des großen Parterres angelegt worden war, wie auf Bellottos Gemälde (Seite 67) links zu sehen ist, wurde 1892 aus sittlichen Gründen abgeholzt.

Die beiden Kammergärten, kurz nach 1750 nach Plänen von Jean Nicolas Jadot angelegt, waren schon zu Maria Theresias Zeiten der kaiserlichen Familie vorbehalten. Um 1770 wurden die eisernen Laubengänge, die heute von Kletterrosen überwuchert werden (Seite 78) und die zierlichen hölzernen Pavillons aufgestellt, deren Deckenmalereien von Schülern oder Mitarbeitern Bergls stammen. Mit den „Bergl"-Zimmern im Erdgeschoß des Schlosses besteht nicht nur dieser zufällige künstlerische, sondern der prinzipielle Zusammenhang, der im Barock zwischen Natur und Architektur herrscht.

73 Pavillon und Rosenhag im Kronprinzengarten vor der Ostfassade. – Das Palmenhaus, errichtet 1881 nach Plänen des Architekten Sengschmid.

Der östliche Kammergarten wird seit etwa 1875 Kronprinzengarten genannt. Damals wurden die ebenerdigen Räume des Ostflügels als Appartement für den Kronprinzen Rudolf (1858–1889) adaptiert. Der westliche blieb seinem Vater, Kaiser Franz Joseph, vorbehalten und wurde weiterhin Kammergarten genannt.

Das Große Palmenhaus ist eine jener Eisenkonstruktionen, die in der zweiten Hälfte des 19. Jahrhunderts als die bedeutendsten technischen Errungenschaften galten und sensationelle Bauwerke wie den Eiffelturm oder das Riesenrad ermöglichten. Die Grundlagen zu solchen Konstruktionen wurden bereits um 1830 in England beim Bau von Gewächshäusern entwickelt.

Im Bereich des Holländischen Gartens gab es auch von Anfang an Treibhäuser, die ebenso wie die Große Orangerie östlich des Schlosses beheizt werden konnten. Zu Beginn des 19. Jahrhunderts bestanden schon mehr als ein Dutzend solcher Glashäuser, die man seit 1869 durch einen Neubau ersetzen wollte. Das Große Palmenhaus, das fast das ganze Areal des Holländischen Gartens einnimmt, wurde schließlich 1881 fertiggestellt. Es enthält die größte Sammlung fremdländischer Pflanzen in Europa.

76 Ausblick aus der Kleinen Galerie: Die Gloriette. Errichtet 1775 nach Plänen Ferdinand von Hohenbergs.

77/105 Trophäen. Bildhauerarbeiten Johann B. Hagenauers im Inneren und an den Treppen der Gloriette.

Die Gloriette ist ein merkwürdiger klassizistischer Kolonnadenbau, dem Namen nach ein „Ruhmestempel", auf der Höhe des Schönbrunner Berges. Sie ist Blickfang für den, der das große Gartenparkett betritt, zugleich aber auch „Belvedere", also Aussichtspunkt, um den weiten, beherrschenden Blick zu genießen, den Johann Bernhard Fischer von Erlach dem ersten Schloßbau zugedacht hat. Die Gloriette wurde nach Plänen des Architekten Ferdinand Hetzendorf von Hohenberg (1733–1816) erst 1775 vollendet, als vorletzter Bau der

73 Pavilion and rose hedge in the "Garden of the Crown Prince" along the east façade of the palace. – The Palm House, designed by the architect Sengschmid, was built in 1881.

The private garden on the east side has been called "Crown Prince's Garden" since 1875. At that time the ground floor apartment of the east wing was adapted for the use of Crown Prince Rudolf (1858–1889). The garden on the west side remained reserved for his father, Emperor Francis Joseph.

The Palm House is an iron construction of the type regarded at the time as a significant technical advance, which made possible such remarkable structures as the Eiffel Tower or Vienna's ferris wheel, the "Riesenrad". The building technique was first developed for greenhouses in England in 1830.

Near the Dutch Garden there were hothouses from the very beginning which, like the large orangery east of the palace, could be heated. At the beginning of the nineteenth century there were more than a dozen such conservatories, which were to be replaced by a single large glasshouse since 1869. The Palm House, which takes up almost all of the Dutch Gardens, was finally completed in 1881 to the plans of the architect Sengschmid.

76 View of the Gloriette from the Small Gallery. The Gloriette, designed by Ferdinand von Hohenberg, was built in 1775.

77/105 Trophies. Sculptures by Johann B. Hagenauer inside and on the stairs of the Gloriette.

The Gloriette, the name of which means "Temple of Honour", is a rather curious neo-classical portico structure surmounting the hill of Schönbrunn. In not only dominates the view from the garden, but serves also as a "belvedere", or vantage point with the kind of commanding view that Fischer von Erlach had intended for the palace itself in his first design.

The Gloriette was built to the plans of the architect Ferdinand Hetzendorf von Hohenberg (1733–1816), and its completion in 1775 makes it the penultimate addition to the garden layout. The columns of the colonnades are said to have been taken from the imperial palace of Neugebäude, which by being on the military road to Hungary was so badly damaged during the "Kurucz" rebellion of 1704 that it was abandoned. The structure is open on all sides, giving it the feeling of expansiveness of a Greek temple. The stucco-work and statues of the inerior are mostly by Benedikt Henrici and imitate ancient works of art.

In a description of Schönbrunn written in 1805, typical of the time in its sentimental and effusive attitude towards nature, it is said of the war trophies created by Johann B. Hagenauer that "the colossal implements of war gathered here, where all around one can see nothing but the blessings of peace, do not make the best impression". – Is it an irony of history that anti-aircraft guns were placed atop the Gloriette in 1918?

73 *Pavillon et roseraie dans le jardin du prince héritier devant la façade orientale. –*
La grande serre à palmiers, construite d'après les plans de l'architecte Sengschmid en 1881.

Le jardin de la Cour situé à l'est est nommé depuis 1875 le jardin du prince héritier. En effet à cette époque, les pièces du rez-de-chaussée avaient été transformées en appartement pour le prince héritier Rodolphe (1858–1889). Le jardin ouest resta réservé à son père, l'empereur François-Joseph et continua à s'appeler le jardin de la Cour.

La grande serre des palmiers est une de ces constructions de fer qui passaient pour être les conquêtes les plus importantes de la technique dans la seconde moitié du 19 ème siècle et qui rendirent possible l'édification de bâtiments sensationnels comme la tour Eiffel ou la grande Roue. Ce genre de construction fut mis au point en Angleterre vers 1830 au cours de la construction de serres.

Il exista aussi depuis le début dans le jardin hollandais des serres qu'il était possible de chauffer de même qu'également la Grande Orangerie à l'est du château. Au commencement du 19 ème siècle, il y avait déjà plus d'une douzaine de serres de ce genre qu'on comptait, depuis 1869, remplacer par un nouveau bâtiment. La grande serre des palmiers qui occupe presque toute la surface du jardin hollandais fut finalement terminée en 1881 d'après les plans de l'architecte Sengschmid. Elle renferme la plus grande collection de plantes étrangères d'Europe.

76 *Vue de la Petite Galerie: la Gloriette. Construite en 1775 d'après les plans de Ferdinand de Hohenberg.*

77/105 *Trophées. Travaux du sculpteur Johann B. Hagenauer à l'intérieur et sur les escaliers de la Gloriette.*

Cette curieuse construction à colonnades néo-classique, au sommet de la colline de Schönbrunn, accroche les regards de celui qui pénètre dans le jardin; elle est aussi un „belvédère", donc un point de vue pour jouir du large panorama qu'on domine et que Fischer von Erlach avait primitivement destiné au château. La Gloriette a été seulement achevée en 1775 d'après les plans de l'architecte Ferdinand Hetzendorf von Hohenberg (1733–1816). Pour les colonnades on a employé, dit-on, des colonnes du château impérial situé sur la route militaire contre la Hongrie et qui fut plusieurs fois dévasté, la dernière fois pendant la révolte des Kurucs de 1704 si bien qu'on l'avait laissé tomber en ruines. Le bâtiment est ouvert de tous les côtés de sorte qu'il nous donne l'impression d'être un temple méditerranéen. Les stucs et les sculptures de l'intérieur dûs pour la plupart à Benedikt Henrici, sont inspirés de modèles de l'Antiquité. Des trophées créés par Johann B. Hagenauer, on disait déjà en 1805 dans une description de Schönbrunn tout à fait caractéristique de l'engouement sentimental pour la nature de l'époque que „des armes monstrueuses ici où on n'aperçoit autour de soi que les bénédictions de la paix ne font pas bonne impression". – Est-ce une ironie de l'histoire qu'en 1918, on ait installé sur la Gloriette des mitrailleuses pour la défense antiaérienne?

artistico casuale, bensí la realizzazione del principio barocco secondo il quale natura ed architettura debbono essere all'unisono.

73 *Padiglione e roseto nel Giardino del Principe ereditario di fronte alla facciata est. –*
La serra di palme costruita nel 1881 secondo i progetti dell'Architetto Sengschmid.

Il giardino ad est, a partire dal 1875, ha preso il nome di „Kronprinzgarten" o giardino del Principe ereditario. A quei tempi i locali furono trasformati in appartamento per il Principe ereditario Rodolfo (1858/59). Il giardino, ad occidente, fu riservato invece al padre, Francesco Giuseppe, e continuò a chiamarsi „Kammergarten".

La Grande Serra delle Palme appartiene a quelle costruzioni di acciaio, che nella seconda metà dell'Ottocento furono fra le più importanti conquiste della tecnica. Grazie ad esse si ebbe la possibilità di costruire monumenti come la Torre Eiffel o la Grande Ruota nel Prater di Vienna. Il criterio fondamentale alla base di queste costruzioni fu sviluppato già intorno al 1830 in Inghilterra per la realizzazione di serre.

Nell'ambito del Giardino Olandese esistevano anche fin dall'inizio delle serre, che potevano essere riscaldate, così come la Grande Orangerie ad est del castello. Ai primi dell'Ottocento esistevano già più di una dozzina di queste serre, che fin dal 1869 si intendeva sostituire con una struttura nuova. La Grande Serra delle Palme, che si estende quasi completamente sul terreno del Giardino Olandese, fu eseguita secondo i progetti dell'Architetto Sengschmid e, finalmente terminata nel 1881. Essa contiene la più grande raccolta di piante esotiche in Europa.

76 *Veduta dalla Piccola Galleria: La Gloriette. Costruita nel 1775 secondo i progetti di Ferdinando von Hohenberg.*

77/105 *Trofei. Le sculture di Johann B. Hagenauer all'interno e sulle scale della Gloriette.*

La Gloriette è uno strano colonnato classicheggiante, un „tempietto", che sorge sulle sommità della collina di Schönbrunn. Attira immediatamente l'attenzione di chi entra nel giardino del castello; è contemporaneamente un „belvedere" da dove si può godere di una vista meravigliosa ed ampia. Già Johann Bernhard Fischer von Erlach aveva in mente di realizzare un tale progetto.

La Gloriette fu costruita su disegno dell'architetto Ferdinando Hetzendorf von Hohenberg (1733–1816) e ultimata nel 1775, penultimo edificio che sorge nel giardino di Schönbrunn. Pare che per i colonnati siano state utilizzate le colonne del castello imperiale di „Neugebäude" situato sulle Heerstrasse in direzione dell'Ungheria. Questo castello, ridotto ormai ad un ammasso di rovine, fu diverse volte danneggiato; l'ultimo colpo glielo inferse la rivoluzione dei Curuczi nel 1704.

La Gloriette è aperta da ogni lato in modo da ricreare l'atmosfera di un tempio meridionale. Gli stucchi e le sculture, che si trovano all'interno, sono opera di Benedetto Henrici, che aveva tenuto presenti i modelli classici.

Opera di Johann B. Hagenauer sono i trofei, che ben esprimono l'amore sentimentale per la natura che era caratteristico di quell'epoca. A questo proposito è interessante riportare quanto è

Schönbrunner Gartenarchitektur. Für die Kolonnaden verwendete man angeblich Säulen des kaiserlichen Schlosses Neugebäude, welches an der Heerstraße gegen Ungarn lag und mehrmals, zuletzt während des Kuruczen-Aufstandes 1704, so beschädigt wurde, daß es dem Verfall preisgegeben war. Das Bauwerk ist nach allen Seiten offen, sodaß es das Raumerlebnis eines südländischen Tempels bietet. Stuck und Skulpturen im Inneren, meist von Benedikt Henrici, sind antiken Vorbildern nachempfunden.

Von den Trophäen, die Johann B. Hagenauer schuf, hieß es schon 1805 in einer Beschreibung Schönbrunns, ganz typisch für die sentimentale Naturschwärmerei, daß „ungeheure Waffenstücke hier, wo man ringsum nichts als die Segnungen des Friedens erblickt, nicht den besten Eindruck machen". – Ist es Ironie der Geschichte, daß auf der Gloriette im Jahre 1918 Maschinengewehre zur Fliegerabwehr aufgestellt wurden?

78   Der Herzog von Reichstadt, Sohn Napoleons I. Gemälde von Carl von Sales, um 1820. (Napoleonzimmer.) – Sein Gartenwagen ist in der Wagenburg zu sehen.

Im März 1810 vermählte sich Napoleon mit der Erzherzogin Maria Louise, der Tochter des Kaisers Franz I. von Österreich; sein Sohn würde den ersten Herrscherhäusern der Welt ebenbürtig sein! An diesen Sohn – Napoleon II. – erinnern zahlreiche Gegenstände, die seine Mutter mit nach Wien brachte, als das Reich des Korsen zusammengebrochen war. Dazu gehört unter anderem der zierliche Kinderwagen, der im Jahre 1812 nach einem Entwurf Antonio Carassis von Tremblay in Paris gebaut worden war, ein Geschenk der Stadt Paris an den Kaiser zur Geburt des Kronprinzen 1812. Von den Franzosen „l'aiglon" – der kleine Adler – genannt, wuchs der Prinz am Hofe seines österreichischen Großvaters auf. Er führte den Titel eines Herzogs von Reichstadt und wurde ängstlich von aller Politik ferngehalten. Am 22. Mai 1832 ist er in jenem Zimmer gestorben, das heute nach seinem Vater benannt wird, angeblich in dessen Bett. Seine Erziehung folgte habsburgischen Traditionen, und so wurde er zur Gartenarbeit und zum Studium der Botanik angehalten. Das hübsche Bildchen des Koblenzer Malers Carl von Sales (1791–1870) erinnert daran.

80   Kaiser Franz Joseph I. in der Galauniform eines österreichischen Feldmarschalls. Gemälde von Anton Einsle, 1848. (Roter Salon.) – Kaiserin Elisabeth in einer großen Robe. Gemälde von Franz Ruß, 1863. (Arbeitszimmer Franz Josephs.)

Der Kaiser hat selbst ein Leben als Soldat und Beamter geführt, er mißtraute Menschen mit schöpferischen Kräften. Obwohl er mit Anerkennung nicht sparte, war er doch zu sehr mit dem Stolz seines Hauses erfüllt, um sich anderen ganz anzuvertrauen. Aus dem Bild von Franz von Matsch (1881–1942) spricht seine Vereinsamung (Seite 110).
Franz Joseph, 1848–1916 Kaiser von Österreich und Apostolischer König von Ungarn, König von Böhmen etc., ist Europas letzter Monarch „von Gottes Gnaden" gewesen, für den Österreicher ist er der alte Kaiser schlechthin. Fast wird darüber vergessen, daß auch er einmal jung war. Mit 18 Jahren bestieg er im Revolutionsjahr 1848 den Thron.

78   Napoleon II, Duc de Reichstadt, son of Napoleon I. Painting by Carl von Sales, c. 1820. (Napoleon Room.) – His garden carriage is exhibited in the Carriage Collection.

In March 1810 Napoleon married Archduchess Maria Louise, the daughter of Francis I of Austria: an act which would confer upon Napoleon's son a rank equal to that of one of the first ruling houses in Europe! Numerous objects brought to Vienna by Maria Louise after the collapse of Napoleon's empire are reminiscent of Napoleon II, his son. Included among them is the elegant garden carriage built in Paris, in 1812, according to plans by Antonio Carassis of Tremblay, a present of the City of Paris to Napoleon on the occasion of the birth of the crown prince in 1812. Called "l'aiglon" – small eagle – by the French, the Prince was reared at the court of his Austrian grandfather. He bore the title of Duke of Reichstadt and was anxiously kept away from all politics. On May 22, 1832 he died in the room named today after his father – allegedly in the latter's bed. Napoleon II's upbringing followed the established Hapsburg traditions. Consequently he was introduced to horticulture and the study of botany, as shown by the charming little painting by Carl von Sales from Coblenz (1791–1870).

80   Emperor Francis Joseph I in the gala uniform of an Austrian field-marshal. Painting by Anton Einsle, 1848. (Red Drawing Room.) – Empress Elizabeth wearing a festive robe. Painting by Franz Russ, 1863. (Francis Joseph's study.)

The emperor was a soldier and bureaucrat who mistrusted creativity. Although generous with his praise, he was too proud of his origins to confide in others. The painting by Franz von Matsch (1881–1942) conveys the emperor's isolation (page 110).
Francis Joseph, from 1848 to 1916 Emperor of Austria and Apostolic King of Hungary, King of Bohemia, etc., was Europe's last monarch "by the grace of God". For Austrians he was simply the "Aged Emperor" almost as though he had never been a young man. At the age of eighteen Francis Joseph relieved his uncle, Ferdinand, who had proved incapable of governing, ascending the throne during the "year of revolutions" in 1848. The official portrait from that year, by Anton Einsle (1801–1871), still hangs in Schönbrunn.
His beautiful wife Elisabeth, a Bavarian Princess, was so incapable of tolerating the ceremonial strictures of the Vienna Court that she withdrew into isolation and later travelled restlessly through all of Europe. She was twenty-six years old at the time of her portrait by Franz Russ (1844–1906). Horses and dogs were her greatest source of pleasure. Her refusal to attend ceremonial festivities made the Vienna Court a court of men.
In executing his power in Austria – since 1866 "Austria-Hungary" – Francis Joseph relied on the loyal bureaucracy and the supranational military forces. For even the youngest lieutenant the uniform was sufficient to gain access to the Emperor, whereas a civilian had to wait until he was either distinguished by a high order or appointed to a high rank.

78   *Le duc de Reichstadt, fils de Napoléon Ier.*
Portrait de Carl von Sales, vers 1820. (Chambre de
Napoléon.) –
On peut voir son phaéton au musée des Voitures impériales.

En mars 1810, Napoléon épousa Marie-Louise, fille de l'empereur
François Ier d'Autriche; de nombreux objets qu'elle rapporta à
Vienne quand l'empire du Corse s'effondra nous font souvenir de
sons fils-Napoléon II. Il y a, entre autres, une jolie voiture d'enfant,
exécutée en 1812 par Tremblay à Paris, d'après un croquis d'Antonio
Carassis - un cadeau de la Ville de Paris à l'empereur pour la naissance du prince héritier en 1812. „L'Aiglon" qui portait le titre de duc
de Reichstadt grandit à la cour de son grand-père autrichien. Il est
mort le 22 mai 1832 dans la chambre nommée aujourd'hui d'après son
père et, parait-il, dans le lit de celui-ci.
Son éducation suivit les traditions habsbourgeoises; on lui fit donc
étudier la botanique et apprendre le jardinage. C'est ce que nous
rappelle le joli petit tableau d'un peintre de Coblence, Carl de Sales
(1791-1870).

80   *L'empereur François-Joseph Ier portant l'uniforme de*
gala d'un feld-maréchal autrichien. Tableau de
Anton Einsle, 1848. (Chambre rouge.) –
L'impératrice Elisabeth en robe de gala. Tableau de
Franz Russ, 1863. (Cabinet de travail de François-Joseph.)

L'empereur a mené une vie de soldat et de fonctionnaire; il se méfiait
des personnes ayant des facultés créatrices. Quoiqu'il n'hésita pas à
reconnaitre les mérites, il était cependant trop imbu de la fierté de sa
Maison pour faire complètement confiance à quelqu'un d'autre. Son
portrait par Franz von Matsch (1881-1942) traduit sa solitude
(page 110).
François-Joseph, empereur d'Autriche et roi apostolique de Hongrie,
roi de Bohême etc. . . . de 1848 à 1916, a été le dernier monarque par
„la grâce de Dieu"; pour l'Autrichien, c'est simplement le vieil
empereur. On oublie presque qu'il fut jeune lui aussi. A 18 ans, il
monta sur le trône l'année de la révolution de 1848. Le portrait
officiel de cette année là est suspendu à Schönbrunn; il est d'Anton
Einsle (1801-1871).
Elisabeth, sa femme, une belle princesse bavaroise, supporta si mal les
contraintes du protocole de la cour qu'elle s'isola et, plus tard,
voyagea sans relâche à travers l'Europe. Le portrait de Franz Russ
(1844-1906) la montre à l'âge de 26 ans. Les chevaux et les chiens
constituaient sa plus grande joie. Elle restait loin des fêtes de la cour
et fit ainsi de la cour de Vienne une cour réservée aux hommes. Le
pouvoir de François-Joseph en Autriche était fondé sur un corps
loyal de fonctionnaires et sur une armée supranationale. L'uniforme
permettait même au plus jeune des lieutenants d'obtenir accès auprès
de l'empereur. Un civil, pour avoir cet honneur, devait attendre
d'obtenir une haute décoration ou d'avoir été nommé conseiller
aulique.

detto in una descrizione di Schönbrunn del 1805: „Le armi
imponenti, collocate in un luogo dove regna la pace e la serenità,
fanno un'impressione molto strana". Ironia della sorte: proprio in
cima alla Gloriette fu installata, nel 1918, una postazione antiaerea.

78   *Il Duca di Reichstadt, figlio di Napoleone I. Dipinto*
di Carl von Sales, intorno al 1820. (Stanza di Napoleone.) –
Il suo carrozzino estivo si può ammirare nel Museo delle
carrozze (Wagenburg).

Nel marzo 1810 Napoleone sposò l'Arciduchessa Maria Luisa, figlia
dell'Imperatore Francesco I d'Austria. In questo modo suo figlio
avrebbe fatto parte, a buon diritto, di una delle maggiori casate del
mondo. Vi sono molti oggetti, portati dalla madre a Vienna dopo la
caduta del grande Corso, che ricordano la presenza di Napoleone II.
Fra questi va menzionata la graziosa culla, costruita a Parigi nel 1812
su disegno di Antonio Carassi di Tremblay, un dono della città di
Parigi all'Imperatore in occasione della nascita del Principe ereditario.
Soprannominato dai francesi „l'aiglon" - l'aquilotto -, il principino
crebbe alla corte del nonno materno. Nonostante fosse Duca di
Reichstadt, fu tenuto lontano da ogni forma di politica. Morì il
22 maggio 1832 in quella stanza che è intitolata oggi a suo padre, forse
addirittura nel di lui letto.
Secondo la tradizione asburgica, per l'educazione di Napoleone II, si
tennero in considerazione tanto il giardinaggio quanto lo studio della
botanica, come si può vedere anche dal quadretto del pittore di
Coblenza, Carlo von Sales (1791-1870).

80   *L'Imperatore Francesco Giuseppe I in alta uniforme*
di un feldmaresciallo austriaco. Dipinto di Anton Einsle,
1848. (Salone rosso.) –
L'Imperatrice Elisabetta in abito di gala. Dipinto di
Franz Russ, 1863. (Studio di Francesco Giuseppe.)

L'Imperatore condusse tutta la sua vita come soldato e impiegato,
senza mai simpatizzare per persone dalle capacità creative. Benchè
mai si risparmiasse nella fatica, era troppo orgoglioso del suo casato
per dar fiducia a terzi. Il pittore Francesco von Matsch (1881-1942) ha
ben raffigurato il suo isolamento (pag. 110).
Francesco Giuseppe, dal 1848 al 1916 Imperatore d'Austria, Re
Apostolico di Ungheria, Re di Boemia ecc. fu, in Europa, l'ultimo
monarca, „per grazia di Dio"; per gli austriaci è semplicemente „il
vecchio Imperatore". Spesso ci si dimentica che anche lui era stato
giovane. A 18 anni, nel 1848, anno dei grandi moti rivoluzionari, salì
al trono. A Schönbrunn si può ammirare il dipinto ufficiale che narra
l'avvenimento di questi anni, opera di Antonio Einsle (1801-1871).
La sua splendida consorte Elisabetta, una Principessa bavarese, non
riuscì a sopportare le dure regole del cerimoniale di corte. Così si
rinchiuse in se stessa e in seguito cominciò a viaggiare, senza pausa,
per l'Europa. Il ritratto di Francesco Russ (1844-1906) ce la mostra
all'età di ventisei anni.
Elisabetta aveva due grandi passioni: i cavalli e i cani. Si asteneva dal
partecipare alle feste della Corte, così che questa divenne, pratica-
mente, esclusività degli uomini.
L'Imperatore fondò il suo potere in Austria (dal 1866 nell'Austria-
Ungheria) su due perni: una schiera di fedeli impiegati e un esercito
sovrannazionale. L'indossare l'uniforme consentiva anche all'ufficiale

Seine schöne Gemahlin Elisabeth, eine bayerische Prinzessin, hat den zeremoniellen Zwang des Hofes so wenig ertragen können, daß sie sich abkapselte und ruhelos durch Europa reiste. Das Porträt von Franz Ruß (1844–1906) zeigt sie im Alter von 26 Jahren. Ihre größte Freude hatte sie an Pferden und Hunden. Den höfischen Festen aber blieb sie fern und machte den Wiener Hof zu einem Hof der Männer. Franz Joseph stützte seine Herrschaft in Österreich – seit 1866 „Österreich-Ungarn" – auf die loyale Beamtenschaft und auf das übernationale Heer. Die Uniform verschaffte selbst dem jüngsten Leutnant den Zutritt zum Kaiser. Ein Zivilist mußte auf diese Ehre warten, bis er einen hohen Orden bekam oder Hofrat wurde.

81   Das Hundertjahr-Jubiläum des Maria-Theresien-Ordens 1857. Der Kaiser auf der Schloßtreppe. Gemälde von Fritz d'Allemand. (Billardzimmer.)

82/83   Festbankett für die Ritter des Maria-Theresien-Ordens in der Großen Galerie des Schlosses. Gemälde von Fritz d'Allemand, 1857. (Billardzimmer.)

Als sich 1857 der Stiftungstag des Militär-Maria-Theresien-Ordens zum hundertsten Male jährte, gab der Kaiser den Offizieren der Wiener Garnison ein Gastmahl im Schloßparterre und den „Theresienrittern" ein Bankett in der Großen Galerie. Fritz d'Allemand hat dieses Ereignis mit Gefühl für die festliche Stimmung und mit großer Kenntnis der Uniformen und Nationalkostüme sowie der Gala-Livreen der Lakaien festgehalten.

106   Napoleons Einzug in Schönbrunn im Mai 1809. Stich von François Aubertin (Ausschnitt).

107   Kaiser Napoleon I. und Kaiserin Marie Luise, geborene Erzherzogin von Österreich. Miniaturen auf Elfenbein von Jean-Baptiste Isabey, 1810.

108   Das Napoleon-Zimmer.

Das Napoleon-Zimmer im östlichen Flügel des Schönbrunner Schlosses trägt seinen Namen vielleicht gar nicht zu Recht, denn es ist nicht genau bekannt, in welchem Zimmer Napoleon während seiner beiden Aufenthalte in Schönbrunn schlief. Jedenfalls bewohnte er jene Räume, die Maria Theresia nach dem Tode ihres Gatten neu einrichten und kostbar ausstatten ließ. Vorher war das sogenannte Napoleon-Zimmer ihr Schlafzimmer gewesen, in dem das Paradebett stand, und somit auch das Geburtszimmer mehrerer ihrer Kinder.
Napoleons Truppen besetzten Wien im November 1805 und der Kaiser der Franzosen zog nach der Schlacht bei Austerlitz im Dezember in Schönbrunn ein, wo er bis zur Unterzeichnung des Friedens von Preßburg blieb, die am 26. Dezember in Schönbrunn erfolgte.
Zum zweitenmal kam Napoleon im Mai 1809 nach Wien und hielt sich etwa ein halbes Jahr in Schönbrunn auf, bis der harte Wiener Frieden im Oktober ausgehandelt war. Damals geschah es, daß während einer Truppenparade, die Napoleon im Ehrenhof abnahm, ein siebzehnjähriger Naumburger ein Attentat versuchte: Der Patriot mußte seine Tat mit dem Leben bezahlen.
Im Napoleon-Zimmer hängen seit 1873 Brüsseler Tapisserien des 18. Jahrhunderts nach Entwürfen von Hyacinthe de la Peigne.

81   The centennial of the founding of the Order of Maria Theresa in 1857. The Emperor descending the palace stairway. Painting by Fritz d'Allemand. (Billiard Room.)

82/83   Banquet in the Great Gallery of Schönbrunn honouring the Knights of the Order of Maria Theresa. Painting by Fritz d'Allemand, 1857. (Billiard Room.)

On the centenary of the founding of the Military Order of Maria Theresa in 1857, the Emperor hosted a banquet in the Large Gallery for the "Knights of Theresa" and a dinner party for the officers of the Vienna garrison on the ground floor. Fritz d'Allemand has both captured the festive atmosphere of the celebration and admirably demonstrated his familiarity with the uniforms and national costumes of the officers as well as the gala-livery of the servants and lackeys.

106   Napoleon's entrée in Schönbrunn in 1809. Engraving by François Aubertin (detail).

107   Emperor Napoleon I and Empress Marie Luise, née Archduchess of Austria. Miniatures on ivory by Jean-Baptiste Isabey, 1810.

108   Napoleon Room.

The Napoleon Room in the east wing of Schönbrunn is perhaps an undeserved designation, as no one knows where Napoleon slept during his two stays in Schönbrunn. It is known that he occupied the same rooms that Maria Theresa had had newly furnished subsequent to the death of her husband, some of which were lavishly decorated. Prior to that, the so-called Napoleon Room had served as her bedroom and the birthplace of many of her children – here the canopied bed had stood.
Vienna was occupied by Napoleon's troops in November 1805, with the Emperor of the French nation installing himself in Schönbrunn following the battle of Austerlitz in December. He remained at Schönbrunn until the Treaty of Pressburg was signed at Schönbrunn palace on the 26th of December. In May 1809, Napoleon came to Vienna a second time and resided at Schönbrunn for half a year, until the Treaty of Vienna had been negotiated in October. During a military parade that Napoleon was receiving in the courtyard parade ground, a seventeen-year-old lad from Naumburg attempted to assassinate the French emperor: the patriot paid for his fervour with his life.
By contrast, there is nothing to remind one of the great conqueror because the room underwent so many alterations. In 1873, the room was furnished for the last time with eighteenth-century Brussels tapestries, woven to the designs of Hyacinthe de la Peigne and depicting scenes from military life.

81 Le centenaire de l'ordre de Marie-Thérèse 1857. L'empereur sur l'escalier du château. Peinture de Fritz d'Allemand. (Salle du billard.)

82/83 Banquet de gala pour les chevaliers de l'ordre de Marie-Thérèse dans la Grande Galerie du château. Tableau de Fritz l'Allemand, 1857. (Salle du billard.)

Lorsqu'en 1857, ce fut le centenaire de la fondation de l'ordre militaire de Marie-Thérèse, l'empereur donna un festin dans le parc du château pour les officiers de la garnison viennoise et un banquet dans la Grande Galerie pour les „officiers de Marie-Thérèse". Fritz d'Allemand a fixé par l'image cet évènement avec beaucoup de sensibilité à l'atmosphère de fête et avec une connaissance admirable des uniformes et costumes nationaux ainsi que des livrées de gala des laquais.

106 Entrée de Napoléon à Schönbrunn en 1809, gravure de François Aubertin (Détail).

107 L'empereur Napoléon Ier et l'impératrice Marie-Louise, née archiduchesse d'Autriche. Miniatures sur ivoire de Jean-Baptiste Isabey, 1810.

108 La chambre de Napoléon.

La chambre de Napoléon, située dans l'aile est du château de Schönbrunn, ne porte peut-être pas son nom à bon droit car on ne sait pas exactement dans quelle chambre Napoléon dormit lors de ses deux séjours à Schönbrunn. Toujours est-il qu'il habita les pièces que Marie-Thérèse avait fait remeubler après la mort de son mari et décorer en partie de façon infiniment précieuse. Auparavant, cette chambre dite de Napoléon avait été la chambre à coucher de Marie-Thérèse où se dressait le lit de parade et donc la chambre où elle mit au monde plusieurs de ses enfants.
Les troupes napoléoniennes occupèrent Vienne en novembre 1805 et, en décembre, après la bataille des Trois empereurs à Austerlitz, l'empereur des Français emménagea à Schönbrunn où il resta jusqu'au 26 décembre, date de la signature à Schönbrunn de la paix de Presbourg. Il vint pour la deuxième fois à Vienne en mai 1809 et séjourna pendant environ 6 mois à Schönbrunn jusqu'à ce que le difficile Traité de Vienne fut enfin réglé en octobre. C'est à cette époque-là qu'un jeune homme de Naumbourg, âgé de 17 ans, attenta à la vie de Napoléon alors que celui-ci assistait à une parade des troupes dans la cour d'Honneur: ce patriote dut payer son action de sa vie.
Dans la chambre de Napoléon, rien par contre ne nous rappelle le conquérant car elle a été plusieurs fois redécorée; la dernière fois (en 1873) on y a tendu des tapisseries de Bruxelles du 18 ème siècle, tissées d'après des cartons d'Hyacinthe de la Peigne et qui représentent des scènes de la vie militaire.

più giovane di conferire coll'Imperatore. Ciò era consentito a un civile solo nel caso dovesse ricevere un'onorificenza superiore o fosse nominato consigliere aulico.

81 Centenario della fondazione dell'ordine di Maria Teresa 1857. L'imperatore sullo scalone del castello. Dipinto di Fritz d'Allemand. (Stanza del bigliardo.)

82/83 Banchetto ufficiale per i cavalieri dell'ordine militare di Maria Teresa nella Grande Galleria del castello. Dipinto di Fritz d'Allemand, 1857. (Stanza del bigliardo.)

Nel 1867, in occasione del centenario dell'istituzione dell'ordine militare di Maria Teresa, l'Imperatore offrì un pranzo, al pianoterra del castello, agli ufficiali della guarnigione di Vienna e un banchetto, nella Grande Galleria, ai cavalieri di Maria Teresa.
Federico d'Allemand ha fissato questo avvenimento ben rappresentando l'atmosfera solenne di questa occasione e dimostrando di avere una conoscenza molto profonda delle uniformi e dei costumi nazionali nonchè delle livree di gala dei lacchè.

106 Ingresso ufficiale a Schönbrunn di Napoleone. Incisione di François Aubertin (Particolare).

107 L'Imperatore Napoleone I e l'Imperatrice Maria Luisa, nata Arciduchessa d'Austria. Miniature su avorio di Jean-Baptiste Isabey, 1810.

108 La stanza di Napoleone.

La stanza di Napoleone, che si trova nell'ala est del castello, porta forse ingiustamente questo nome in quanto non è affatto certo che l'Imperatore dei Francesi vi sia stato ospitato durante i suoi due soggiorni a Schönbrunn. E' comunque cosa sicura che abitò in quelle stanze che Maria Teresa, dopo la morte del marito, aveva fatto rinnovare e arredare, in parte, preziosamente. La stanza cosiddetta di Napoleone era stata prima la camera da letto di Maria Teresa: là si trovava un letto sontuoso. In questo locale vennero alla luce alcuni dei suoi figli.
Le truppe di Napoleone avevano occupato Vienna nel novembre del 1805; l'Imperatore dei Francesi, dopo la battaglia di Austerlitz, nel dicembre dello stesso anno, si insediò a Schönbrunn, dove rimase fino alla firma del trattato di pace di Bratislava, che ebbe luogo appunto a Schönbrunn il 26 dicembre. Napoleone venne, per la seconda volta, a Vienna nel maggio 1809 e vi si trattene per circa sei mesi, fino cioè alla firma della dura pace di Vienna, nel mese di ottobre dello stesso anno. In questa occasione avvenne che, durante una parata, nel cortile d'onore, un giovane di diciassette anni, originario di Naumburg, attentasse alla vita di Napoleone. Il giovane patriota pagò questo atto con la propria vita.
Nella stanza di Napoleone vi sono, sin dal 1873, delle tapezzerie di Bruxelles, eseguite su progetto di Hyacinthe de la Peigne.

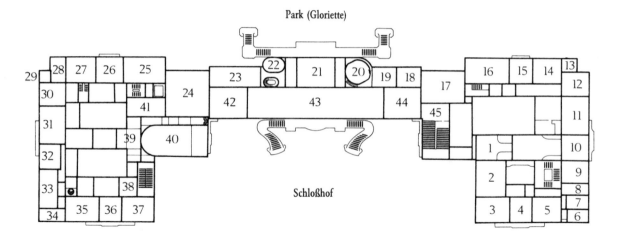

Park (Gloriette)

Schloßhof

1	Gardezimmer	Guardroom	Salle des gardes	Stanza della guardia
2	Billardzimmer	Billiard Room	Salle du billard	Stanza del bigliardo
3	Nußbaumzimmer	Walnut Room	Salon en noyer	Stanza di noce
4	Arbeitszimmer Franz Josephs I.	Franz Joseph I's Study	Cabinet de travail de François-Joseph Ier	Studio di Francesco Giuseppe I
5	Schlafzimmer Franz Josephs I.	Franz Joseph I's Bedroom	Chambre à coucher de François-Joseph Ier	Camera da letto di Francesco Giuseppe I
6	Terrassenkabinett West	West Terrace Room	Le cabinet de la terrasse ouest	Stanzetta con terrazza – Ovest
7	Stiegenkabinett	Staircase Room	Le cabinet de l'escalier	Stanzino-scale
8	Toilettezimmer	Powder Closet	Le cabinet de toilette	Toeletta
9	Schlafzimmer	Bedroom	Chambre à coucher	Stanza da letto
10	Salon der Kaiserin	Empress's Drawing-Room	Salon de l'impératrice Elisabeth	Salone dell'Imperatrice
11	Maria-Antoinette-Zimmer	Maria Antoinette Room	Salon de Marie-Antoinette	Maria Antonietta-Stanza
12	Kinderzimmer	Children's Room	Chambre des enfants	Stanza dei bambini
13	Frühstückszimmer	Breakfast Room	Salle du petit déjeuner	Stanza della prima colazione
14	Gelber Salon	Yellow Drawing-Room	Salon jaune	Salone giallo
15	Balkonzimmer	Balcony Room	Salle au balcon	Stanza con balcone
16	Spiegelsaal	Mirror Room	Salle des Glaces	Salone degli specchi
17	Großes Rosa-Zimmer	"Large Rosa" Room	Grand salon de Rosa	Stanza grande di Rosa
18	1. Kleines Rosa-Zimmer	First "Small Rosa" Room	Premier petit salon de Rosa	1. Stanza piccola di Rosa
19	2. Kleines Rosa-Zimmer	Second "Small Rosa" Room	Deuxième petit salon de Rosa	2. Stanza piccola di Rosa
20	Chinesisches Rundkabinett	Round Chinese Room	Cabinet chinois rond	Stanzetta cinese rotonda
21	Kleine Galerie	Small Gallery	Petite Galerie	Piccola galleria
22	Ovales Chinesisches Kabinett	Oval Chinese Room	Cabinet chinois ovale	Stanzetta cinese ovale
23	Rösselzimmer	"Rössel" Room	Salon des Chevaux	Stanza dei cavalli
24	Zeremoniensaal	Ceremonial Hall	Salle des Cérémonies	Sala delle cerimonie
25	Blauer Chinesischer Salon	Blue Chinese Drawing-Room	Salon chinois bleu	Salotto cinese azzurro
26	Vieux-Laque-Zimmer	"Vieux-Laque" Room	Salon Vieux-Laque	Stanza vieux-laque
27	Napoleonzimmer	Napoleon Room	Chambre de Napoléon	Stanza di Napoleone
28	Porzellanzimmer	Porcelain Room	Salon des Porcelaines	Stanza delle porcellane
29	Miniaturenkabinett	Miniatures Room	Le cabinet des miniatures	Stanzetta delle miniature
30	Millionenzimmer	Millions Room	Le salon des Millions	Stanza dei milioni
31	Gobelinsalon	"Gobelin" Room	Le salon des Gobelins	Stanza degli arazzi
32	Gedenkzimmer	Memorial Room	Salle commémorative	Stanza delle rimembranze
33	Roter Salon	Red Drawing-Room	La chambre rouge	Salone rosso
34	Terrassenkabinett Ost	East Terrace Room	Le cabinet de la terrasse est	Stanzetta con terrazza – Est
35	Geburtszimmer	Natal Room	Chambre natale	Sala parto
36	Arbeitszimmer Erzhzg. Franz Karls	Archduke Franz Karl's Study	Le cabinet de travail de l'archiduc François-Charles	Studio dell'Arciduca Francesco Carlo
37	Salon Erzhzg. Franz Karls	Archduke Franz Karl's Drawing-Room	Le salon de l'archiduc François-Charles	Salone dell'Arciduca Francesco Carlo
38	Wildschweinzimmer	"Wild Boar" Room	La salle des sangliers	Stanza dei cinghiali
39	Durchgangszimmer	Corridor	Salle de passage	Stanza di passaggio
40	Schloßkapelle	Chapel	Chapelle du château	Cappella
41	Maschinenzimmer	Machinery Room	Salle des machines	Stanza delle macchine
42	Karussellzimmer	Carousel Room	Salon du Carrousel	Stanza del carosello
43	Große Galerie	Great Gallery	Grande Galerie	Grande galleria
44	Laternenzimmer	Lantern Room	Salle des Lanternes	Stanza delle lanterne
45	Blaue Stiege	Blue Staircase	Escalier bleu	Scala azzurra

STAMMTAFEL DES HAUSES ÖSTERREICH

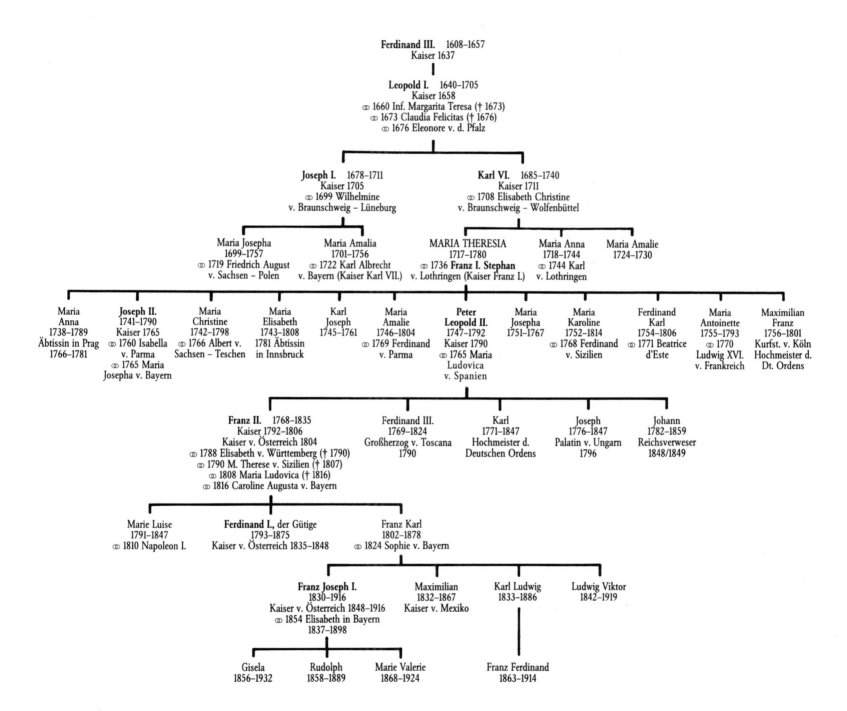

Bildnachweis

Gerhard Trumler, Wien: 1, 2, 10, 15, 16, 25, 43, 45–48, 51 oben, 53–61, 62 links und unten, 63, 64 rechts, 65, 67 unten, 68–77, 78 unten, 79, 93–96, 105, 106 oben, 110 (Historisches Museum der Stadt Wien), 111, 112

Akademische Druck- und Verlagsanstalt, Graz: 51 unten, 78 oben links

Bundesdenkmalamt, Wien: 32 unten

Graphische Sammlung Albertina: 7

Heeresgeschichtliches Museum, Wien: 49 unten

Kunsthistorisches Museum, Wien (Foto Mayer): 8, 9, 12, 13, 26–30, 32 oben, 39, 41, 42, 44, 49 oben, 50, 52, 62 oben, 66, 67 oben, 78 oben rechts, 80–84, 106 unten, 107

Österreichische Nationalbibliothek, Bildarchiv: 31, 64 links, 108, 109